T0086195

BE STILL:
A JOURNEY OF THE HEART

NOAH REESE

WESTBOW
PRESS®
A DIVISION OF THOMAS NELSON
& ZONDERVAN

WestBow Press books may be ordered through booksellers or by contacting:

WestBow Press
A Division of Thomas Nelson & Zondervan
1663 Liberty Drive
Bloomington, IN 47403
www.westbowpress.com
844-714-3454

ISBN: 978-1-9736-9857-9 (sc)
ISBN: 978-1-9736-9858-6 (hc)
ISBN: 978-1-9736-9856-2 (e)

Library of Congress Control Number: 2023910201

Print information available on the last page.

WestBow Press rev. date: 05/20/2023

"You make known to me the path of life; in your presence, there is fullness of joy; at your right hand are pleasures forevermore." (Psalm 16:11)

Nothing compares with the presence of the Lord. We were created for intimacy with Him. God is always with us, the Spirit of God in us as a guarantee of our glorious eternity when we surrender our lives to Jesus as both our Savior from sin and our Master for eternity.

Then there is also the tangible, life-changing, kingdom-building presence of God. This is the presence that allowed Peter to walk down a street and people in the vicinity of the presence were healed (Acts 5:15). This presence permeated a piece of Paul's clothing, bringing healing and freedom from demonic oppression (Acts 19:12). This is the presence where the Holy Spirit manifests himself through intimacy and communion. The pleasure found in a young daughter cuddled in her Dad's arms, or a hurt child comforted by his mother's embrace. Intimacy. Relationship. The heart of our adoring and loving Father.

I believe the Lord's intentions with these devotionals are to open our hearts to hear his voice of spirit and truth and to lead us into his presence to encounter the Spirit of God. So that we may know his heart and be transformed.

Henri Nouwen says solitude is the furnace of transformation. We must create margin in our hearts and minds for digesting spirit and truth. There must be space in our thoughts to be still before the Lord.

If we never train our hearts and minds to bow to the Lord, we will never hear his transforming whisper or feel his healing touch.

He is constantly thrilled to be with us and more excited than we are to share his heart with us and wrap us up in his big loving arms.

So here in this place, train to be still. Train to be aware of the Holy Spirit. Come with expectation. Come with joy. Come with brokenness and sin. Come with guilt and shame. Now lay them at the feet of Jesus and join him on a journey of the heart.

The Process: Be still and know that he is God (Psalm 46:10). Take a moment to prepare your heart and mind to be with the Father each day prior to reading. Use one of the following verses, or another verse God has given you. Speak it aloud, repeatedly, softly, slowly, and allow the spirit and truth of the Scripture to permeate and cleanse your heart and mind of distractions, ushering you into the heart of the Father.

Unless otherwise noted, all scripture referenced is in the English Standard Version (ESV).

> I am still and I know that you are God (Psalm 46:10)
>
> You are my Lord, I have no good apart from you (Psalm 16:11)
>
> My heart is glad and my whole being rejoices (Psalm 16:9)
>
> The Lord is my Shepherd (Psalm 23:1)
>
> Where the Spirit of the Lord is there is freedom (2 Corinthians 3:17)
>
> God is my refuge and my strength (Psalm 46:1)
>
> I will taste and see that the Lord is good (Psalm 34:8)
>
> The Lord is near to the brokenhearted and saves the crushed in spirit (Psalm 34:18)
>
> The Lord redeems the life of his servants (Psalm 34:22)

Now be still and know that he is God for two minutes. Read through the devotional. Be aware of the Holy Spirit, and be open to hearing him speak. Write down what 'sticks out', what comes to mind, what applies to a current situation, what the Father is saying. Then spend another two minutes in silence to digest, process, to be with God. That is it.

A Prayer for You: We say, Lord, you are our Lord; we have no good thing apart from you. Holy Spirit come, fill our hearts with a fresh hunger, a burning for you. We want to be with you. Holy Spirit lead me into all truth. Increase my power of discernment, by constant practice, to distinguish good from evil (Heb. 5:13). Tune my heart to hear, know, and obey your voice.

Let your love flood my heart through your Spirit (Rom 5:5) now oh Lord. Drive away doubt, drive out fear, and drive away the anxiety. Holy Spirit you are here, so I am in a place of freedom, and your freedom reigns in my life. Thank you. Thank you. Thank you …

So we begin … a journey of the heart …

CONTENTS

1

THE CORE

We each have a calling, a destiny, a mission, a specific purpose for which we were created. Primarily, it is to glorify our Maker and Father, the almighty God. Within this, we each have this specific calling. For Moses, it was the rescue of the Israelites, God's people, and he had over forty years of preparation. For Noah, it was the ark, the carrying on of the human race, and this did not take place until later in his life (between five hundred and six hundred years old). John the Baptist's mission, the peak of it, took place in a six-month time span. Jesus was unknown for the first thirty years of His life, and then God used Him incredibly for three years, which changed the entire world.

We do not stand idly by as we watch and wait in excited anticipation for God's purpose and plan to unfold in our lives. We pursue Him. We decrease so that He may increase. We surrender and submit. We open the door when He knocks. We obey. We love. We live. We live abundantly. We do not compare to others. This life is between you and God, me and God. Whatever takes place outside that is for His purposes, for the Great Commission, not for our personal gain, comfort, stardom, feelings of success, or superiority.

What would our lives look like if we lived every waking moment as if the only person who really mattered was God? What if we lived like His purpose for us on this earth was the most important thing we could ever accomplish?

We would prepare! We would need to know the goals of our Commander—how He operates and His historical ways of executing His plans. We would mold ourselves to His likeness to better fulfill and accomplish the mission when the time comes. We would train physically, for this has some value, but more so for godliness. We would train hard. We would train through blood, sweat, and tears. We would be single-minded, focused, undistracted.

When the time comes, when the trumpets sound, when the race begins, when the fight ensues, when God's time for us arrives, we will be ready! We will be weak in ourselves so that we are insanely strong in Christ. We will be full of the Spirit so that love, grace, and power burst and explode out from every word and action.

And all for what? To expand His kingdom? To display Christ to a lost world? Yes, but ultimately to bring joy, love, and glory to the Most High God, the Alpha and the Omega, the Ultimate Warrior and Unmatched Lover, the Beginning and the End. Our Master, our Friend, our Father. The Great I Am!

2

REST

est in the Lord and you will find peace. Resting in the Lord is like participating in your favorite activity, like watching a beautiful sunset where you are captivated by the beauty, and if for but a moment, all else fades away. In the midst of the sunset, the colors, lines, clouds, sun, and sky capture every thought. At that moment there is no worry, no anxiety over deadlines or expectations. There is no concern for the future or finances or even family. Your full and undivided attention is gladly immersed in the beauty of that moment, the beauty of that sunset where all else fades away.

In rest, we are so enamored with God, confident in His abounding love and grace over us, certain of His plans and purposes, that we melt into His goodness. The world fades away, leaving behind no thought of the present troubles or future worries. In rest, we find Jesus in intimacy. In rest, we let go of what we so desperately feel we need to hold on to at that moment, in that season of life.

We take Jesus at His word; we actually believe Him when He offers for the tired, burdened, and weary to come to Him so He will give them rest. We accept His yoke that is easy and His burden that is light, but only after we lift our own burdens and yokes off our shoulders and heave them down at the feet of Jesus. In rest, it is as though we defy gravity because we are weightless.

To be still and know that He is God is to live free from the weights and burdens of the world, the devil, and ourselves. We rest in supreme confidence that our God has already overcome the world. We rest in utter peace that our heavenly Father is greater than he who is in the world. In rest, we abandon independence and fall into a beautiful, life-giving dependence on the Holy Spirit.

To be still and know that He is God is also to know that we are not God. It is to know that the devil is not God. To know that He is God is a revelation that can only be found in a place of rest and stillness before the Father where all else fades away. Yes, every distraction, every to-do item, and every deadline and stressor that comes to mind is swept away or written down so that you can release it, knowing it will not be forgotten for later.

Wait patiently for the Lord. Rest is a discipline that is used as a weapon. Rest only occurs in Christ, but we must train our hearts and minds to join Him. He longs to abide with us in rest. He honors us with His gift of peace that guards our hearts and minds in Him, sweeping us into a euphoric state of rest only experienced in His presence. His presence changes everything. In His presence, in the shelter of His wings, in His abounding mercy and love, we are invited into His heart, where rest, our supreme confidence in His eternal goodness in every situation, floods our hearts and minds.

Rest is not about us as much as it is about honoring and glorifying God through a complete trust in Him. When we cannot find rest, it is because we choose to make the problems, people, and circumstances in our lives bigger than God. We glorify God in rest. We have in us the Holy Spirit: our comforter, our guide, our helper and friend, who draws us to Jesus; glorifies Jesus; brings power from on high; and is a Spirit of love, power, and self-control, never fear or timidity. He, the Holy Spirit, brings love, demonstrations of the power of our God, and deep conviction. We have in us the same Spirit who raised Jesus from the dead. He leads us into all truth and reminds us of Jesus's words. He convicts of sin and pours out His fruit over us (love, joy, peace, patience, kindness, goodness, gentleness, faithfulness, and self-control).

Jesus had to leave so the Holy Spirit could come and fill us afresh every day through our submission and surrender to Him and the ministry he is bringing, his life in and through us from the Father. Rest in the Holy Spirit. Ask Him to come and join you in this moment. Ask Him to speak to you. Make known to Him how much you want to know Him and see Him glorify Jesus in your life. Wait on the Holy Spirit to flood you with the peace Jesus has gifted to us. In our broken and contrite hearts, there is a greater reciprocating reaction in heaven that does not match but supersedes our choice to recklessly abandon all to trust in Jesus.

A broken and contrite heart the Lord will not despise. In humility, we know our place before the Lord; He is God over everything and everyone, and our sole purpose on this earth is to bring glory, honor, and praise to the name of Jesus, crying out, "Abba Father!" In this place, we find the rest that outlasts the enemy. Rest that demolishes strongholds and counters the flesh. Rest that is too peaceful and patient for the enemy to endure. Rest that quiets our spirits to hear the voice of the Holy Spirit. Rest that refreshes our spirits as the world around us fades away and no longer holds power over us. Let the world fade away, and take refuge in the Almighty's wings—that is, abide in Jesus, the author and perfecter of our faith.

Breathe the Spirit in and breathe out the anxious worries of this world. Inhale the Holy Spirit to flow through the caverns of your soul, and exhale the false stressors that the flesh and enemy place on us. Pray as if it all depends on God, and live as if it all depends on you. You had a blood transfusion with Jesus. He breathes out; we breathe in. He is our everything. He is all that we need. He is our rest, our peace, our eternal salvation.

3

PAIN

One learns of the pain of others by suffering one's
own pain, by turning inside one's self, by finding
one's own soul. And it is important to know of
pain. It destroys our self-pride, our arrogance, and
our indifference toward others. It makes us aware
of how frail and tiny we are and of how much we
must depend on the Master of the Universe.

—Chaim Potok, The Chosen

My career is in fact for my family, and we have seasons
and levels of pain that destroy our flesh and the works
of the devil. They create a humility in our sorrow
and frustration that forces us to focus inward rather than on our
constant distractions of the world, technology, luxuries, other
people, and even comfort and advancement of self.

This pain stops the ever-running train of busyness and self-
indulgence. We long for and embrace someone or something
more than ourselves, which opens us up in holy vulnerability to
a childlike faith to receive from the Lord. It's only in pain that we
concede our own greatness and say, "God, I need you."

It is in pain that our love and concern for others will bubble up from the depths of Jesus's love in us to create an ever-flowing spring of loving-kindness and genuine care for others who experience pain.

It is in pain that we learn compassion first hand. We then more readily extend it to those around us. It is only through experience that we can speak with authority and state in confidence the lessons learned and their lasting effects.

It is through the pain that we truly depend on our Lord and Savior and see him at His best: in the pouring out of freedom from self, receiving love and grace to receive His gifts to serve Him and others in the midst of our own turmoil. His comfort and peace that guards our hearts and minds allow us to be joyful always and give thanks in all circumstances.

It is through pain that our faith is tested producing a steadfast heart, leading us to maturity in Him (James 1:2-4). It is through Jesus's love and grace over us in times of pain that we learn about Him through experience. We come to know Him, more than just about Him, by perception through time spent in His presence.

It is in pain that the Gospel of Jesus becomes real in our lives so we might serve as witnesses to others of his great and mighty love. To tell the message through self-testimony that Christ alone saves. That Christ alone gives peace, comfort, and rest in the midst of the chaos and pain in and all around us.

So it is in pain that we see hope. A hope that we might decrease and he might increase. A hope that the pain a loved one is enduring will leave them more like Jesus Christ. A hope that in pain we might have the honor of comforting those we love, those we like, or those we hate; or receive comfort from the same.

We wait patiently before the Lord (Psalm 37:7). We still ourselves and know that He is God (Psalm 46:10), our Refuge, our Strength and Stronghold, our Hope, and our Salvation. He is our Strong Deliverer.

4

THE PATH TO
UNDERSTANDING

Often we seek to understand something or someone first before we can move forward. Understanding is the goal so we can obtain information to share with and explain to others. Sometimes our path to understanding is misunderstood. Proverbs 3:5-6 says, "Trust in the Lord with all your heart and do not lean on your own understanding, in all your ways acknowledge him and he will make straight your paths."

To acknowledge God is to know him through experience. Understanding comes through experiencing God. It cannot be the primary focus. Knowledge becomes truth through experience.

It is deep in the heart of the Father, in intimacy, where He gives us encounters and experiences with him that lead us into truth and grant us new perspectives, new ways of thinking.

It is in a heart-to-heart connection with the Father we are transformed through the renewing of our minds. This is not a result of the pursuit of understanding through information.

The path to understanding leads us into the heart of the Father where he experientially reveals truth that grows in our hearts. As we dwell in and experience the goodness of God in this place, we become transformed through a shift in how we think, a renewing of our mind. This experiential truth unveils the Father's heart for us and our circumstances, and we see differently, think differently, and speak differently. This path has led us to a place of understanding.

And we all, with unveiled faces, beholding the glory of the Lord, are being transformed into the same image from one degree of glory to another. For this comes from the Lord who is the Spirit (2 Corinthians 3:18).

The understanding we seek comes through transformation, not information. This never negates the necessity of information, rather it shifts the source of the power we seek and pursue. The kingdom of God does not consist in talk, but in power (1 Corinthians 4:20).

Information is not the focus or the final goal, rather it's an essential instrument the Spirit uses to accompany and ground his transformative work in our lives.

The Lord is my Shepherd, I shall not want (Psalm 23:1). Rather than attempting a better understanding of this passage through information, we speak this as a repetitive prayer and declaration. As these beautiful words begin to penetrate our hearts through the working of the Holy Spirit, we experience the Lord as our Shepherd in our marriage, our family, our work, our church. The Holy Spirit activates the truth and power of the Lord as our Shepherd in our everyday lives.

Fear, doubt, and uncertainty melt away as we are transformed by the renewing of our minds through the experiential truth of the Lord is our Shepherd.

Where the Spirit of the Lord is there is freedom (2 Corinthians 3:17). Where the Spirit of the Lord is there is freedom from addiction, fear, bitterness, un-forgiveness, rage, jealousy, anxiety. Where the Spirit of the Lord is there is freedom from insecurity, doubt, lies, oppression, depression, and demonic influence. Where the Spirit of the Lord is there is freedom ...

5

TWO SIDES TO EVERY COIN

L et's get this idea out of our heads that it is feminine to love; that we are less of a man when we display mercy, compassion, and loving-kindness. The thought that we were created to be lovers of God and man does not take away from the warrior side that God has created in each of His sons.

Jesus had mercy on the blind and broken; compassion on the sinners and the children. He spoke often of His love for His Father and others. Jesus also never backed down when He saw His Father moving. He never cowered from confrontation when it was His Father's will. He stood up for the oppressed, He beat and ran men out of God's house who blasphemed it. He endured more physical, psychological, and spiritual torture than many of us ever will.

There are two sides to every coin. One does not take away from the other. They are joined.

It is heart and heroics, the lover and the fighter, the bringer of life and the deliverer of death. King David wrote poetry and poured out his heart and emotions. Society would call him a fruitcake, weak, feminine. God called him a man after His own heart (1 Samuel 13:14, Acts 13:22). The other side of that coin is King David the warrior who slew tens of thousands (1Sam 18:7,

21:11, 29:5), who danced for God unashamed in the streets (2 Samuel 6:14, 16, 20-22). He was a lover and a fighter.

We must love and we must fight. There is a war and we are called to fight for our hearts as men, for our families, for our friends, for those we live and work with, and for the kingdom of heaven. So here is the paradox, the disconnect, the side of the coin that our society rejects. Here is what Satan wants us to never accept, believe, or find boldness in. We wage our wars with LOVE. (John 13:35) God's LOVE ... God IS Love (1 John 4:16b), and the greatest of all is love (1 Corinthians 13:13, 13:1a).

There is no fear in love (1 John 4:18). There is immeasurable power in love. When we love, God lives in us and His love is made complete in us (1 John 4:12). He is able to do immeasurably more than we could ask or imagine according to the power that is at work within us (Ephesians 3:20), His LOVE. All things birth from Love (John 3:16).

Yes, to live in God's love makes us aliens here in this world (Ephesians 2:19), never to be understood (Matthew 13:14, 13:19) or accepted (John 14:17, John 17:14). To live in God's love is to nail down our citizenship in heaven, not on earth (Ephesians 2:19). Society doesn't know what a man really is, nor do those who scoff at the heart of our Lord, which is composed of meekness, humility, love, mercy, a hunger and thirst for righteousness, purity, joy, unity, and peace (Matthew 5:3-12).

So will you fight? Not as the world does and not with the weapons the world uses (2 Corinthians 10:3-4), but with the unfathomable power of Christ birthed from love (John 3:16, Ephesians 3:18)?

There are two sides to every coin, and we are called to pursue both. We are called to stand side by side, shield to shield, elbow to elbow, with each other as we venture down the narrow path together that our Almighty God has set before us.

For when we lay down our pride, when we lay down our earthly view of God, heaven, and men, then we will become, to society, the losers and the freaks. Those who can't operate, who don't think straight, whose lives are wasted in pipe dreams and fantasies. We are the delusional ones who will be laughed at by those who are lost. GOOD (Matthew 5:11, Luke 6:22)!

For the cross is foolishness to those who are perishing, but to us, it is the power of Christ (1 Corinthians 1:18). We walk tall in a confidence the world will never know (Hebrews 4:16, 10:14, Ephesians 3:12, 1John 3:21). A boldness that intimidates the bullies of the world (Proverbs 28:1). A courage that bewilders the so-called men of the world (2 Timothy 1:7). We run in love that inspires the hurt and compassion that raises up the broken. The light emanating from our very beings (Matthew 5:14-16) blinds the enemy and his feeble warriors. Mountains melt (Psalm 97:5), every knee shall bow and every voice will declare to the heavens that Jesus Christ is Lord (Isaiah 45:23). Our lives bring roars of thunderous joy in heaven as the enemy is slain through loving-kindness and Christ is lifted up through daily acts of obedience. All for His glory.

Everything we are or ever will be is solely for the glory of God. Today we make a choice to declare it, to walk in it, to claim it, to recognize that a life not lived in and for God's love is worthless (John 15:5) and empty, sad and desperate (Mark 3:29). It is mundane and boring, ineffective and cowardly. This world and its desires pass away, but the man who does the will of God lives forever (1 John 2:17).

6

RELENTLESS

God is relentless.

When he sets out to give us his fullness to be like Christ in an area of our lives, then he does so relentlessly; intensifying our experiences in him with the ultimate goal that we become that aspect of God's nature. He teaches us incarnationally in that we become the embodiment of Jesus. We become so much like Jesus that we are his nature in that area that he glorifies in us.

God brings experience after experience, pouring out his nature time and again. Through this process, we learn that he wants to teach us peace (for example), then he begins to teach us how peace becomes truth in our lives, through experience. To know of peace is what most pursue, and they stop there.

But our God is relentless.

His desire is for us to know peace by experience. That means we must go through storms, stressful times, doubt, anxiety, etc. We learn by experience. Through these times, it is glorious as Christ pours out his peace which we cannot even comprehend. Yet it will, if we allow it, block out the world, flesh, and enemy so that our focus remains on him and him alone. We experience his peace.

Our God is relentless.

He does not stop there. Again and again, until over time and experience, we have peace more often, in more circumstances, quicker. We come to a place in our circumstances where we can quickly set our eyes on what is eternal and stand in peace. Then he keeps going because our God is relentless to bring his fullness, not just a measure.

The incarnational way that he teaches and moves brings us to a place in Jesus where we become peace. We are the embodiment of peace, tranquility, and rest. We do not need to seek peace because it runs through our veins, deep in our hearts, bones, and mind. It does not take conscious thought in most circumstances to be at peace because it has become a part of who we are, God's nature flowing through us.

God's nature becomes like a second color of sand in a half-filled jar. When he pours his nature into us, whatever he chooses to teach us, then it's mixed with our true persona and becomes who we are, our identity, and then our promises and inheritance in Christ. It is a promise God makes in our lives and he never breaks a promise. There is no separating it out; he has experientially changed us forever.

Our God is great, wonderful, merciful, compassionate, majestic, and always, constantly, relentless for us.

7

THE ART OF TEMPTATION

"Why do you not understand what I say? It is because you cannot bear to hear my word. You are of your father, the devil, and your will is to do your father's desire. He was a murderer from the beginning and does not stand in the truth, because there is no truth in him. When he lies, he speaks out of his own character, for he is a liar and the father of lies" (John 8:43-44).

The enemy uses layers of lies that operate like a false lens in front of our eyes, and as a cloak in our minds, covering the truth of the Father. The enemy targets the way we see ourselves, how we think about ourselves, the way we see God, how we perceive Him; our circumstances and people around us, how we receive from them, and see them.

False views about ourselves sew shame and guilt, creating a heavy cloud that rests on us and weighs us down. They are a weight that steals our joy and peace in believing in the hope of Jesus Christ. He creates uncertainty and confusion. He targets known areas of weakness and areas of past sins and struggles.

The art of temptation is to steal, kill, and destroy without the victim ever realizing it is taking place. When the perceived destruction, which is a lie, appears to be truth birthed in the mind and heart of the follower of Jesus, then they believe it is their sin, their problem and issue, their guilt and shame. They take ownership of the lie, however small it may be.

In the art of temptation, the enemy sews a kernel of truth, or something very close to one, to convince us of the ploy, to create ownership, and establish condemnation. He loves to condemn us through lies we perceive to be our own thoughts, of which we then take ownership. We must recognize these false lenses and cloaks that he puts in front of us and throws over our minds for what they are.

The longer they linger the more ingrained and influential they become. He initiated them, but if we respond and dwell, even agree with them and begin to act on them, then we invite a foothold in that place of our lives. We must take every thought captive and make them obedient to Christ (2 Cor. 10:5). When we take these lies that are so very tempting to embrace and lay them at the foot of the cross declaring the truth of Jesus, then we create a crack in the lens and a tear in the cloak.

Initially, it is just enough to confirm something is off. We identify the lie and truth is revealed, though we may not truly comprehend at this point. We can now hear the voice of Jesus and his Spirit in that place and in that circumstance. Identification and recognition are our special reconnaissance, our discernment, that initiate putting on the whole armor of God that we may be able to stand against the schemes of the devil (Eph. 6:11).

The truth, the crack in the lie, settles us into the peace of God, which transcends our understanding and guards our hearts and minds in Christ Jesus (Phil 4:7). The enemy's goal in temptation is to sever our communion with God and divide our relationship with others. He pours fuel on the fires that arise daily. He turns a small flame into a seemingly blazing fire by lying, exaggeration, and creating anxiety.

The Devil loves to get us stressed because he can steal our joy through doubt, worry, fear, and anxiety. He will compound small issues until we are no longer seeing Jesus in people or situations. Rather, we are frantically attempting to put out the small, insignificant fires he soaks in fuel. The Art of Temptation is deception for division.

So we, if but for a moment, rest in the Spirit, we can step back, identify, and recognize the false views and ways of thinking. We declare alignment with Jesus (1 Corinthians 2:16b), moving into transformation through the renewing of our minds (Rom 12:1) and a fresh perspective to see Jesus.

Rejoice in the Lord always; be anxious for nothing for He IS WITH YOU! Living by faith is knowing He is with us even when we do not see Him or feel His presence. Ask and declare your needs and desires to God. Claim His truths and promises in your life. Then enter into His peace that is incomprehensible, but guards our hearts and minds in Christ.

Identify and recognize the lie, rejoice, talk to God, step into His peace, and meditate on what is true, honorable, just, pure, lovely, commendable, whatever is excellent and worthy of praise (Philippians 4:4-8).

We fight and counter the enemy from a place of victory (1 Corinthians15:57, Romans 8:37, John 16:33), so the question is never will we overcome, but when will we step into the victory of the Way, the Truth, and the Life he has already won?

8

RADICAL LIVES FOR
RADICAL PARENTING

To be the parents to our children that our Lord created us to be is to do so in a radically different way than the world. Our children must be radically different from their peers; they must live radical lives for Jesus Christ. This begins with you and me. We must first be radical followers of Christ. We must delight in the Lord and be the greatest example of Christ our children see. We will live out Christ as our King at home. We will lead our families against the flow of society in every way possible.

The Lord disciplines those He loves and punishes His children (Hebrews 12:6). If he does not discipline us, and if we do not discipline, then we, and likewise our children, are illegitimate and not true sons and daughters (Hebrews 12:8).

God does not call us to love as the world does and that includes our children. We must train them up in the way of Christ and when they are older, they will not depart (Proverbs 22:6). No discipline seems pleasant at the time, but painful. Later on, however, it produces a harvest of righteousness and peace for those who have been trained by it (Hebrews 12:11).

God has given us the responsibility and the authority to teach, train, rebuke, discipline, and love our children. However, we do this through the Father's love without exasperating them. We do this just as our Father does these things for us. Does our Father give us everything we ask for? No, and many times that is because we ask for the wrong reasons, for our own personal gain and pleasures (James 4:3). Then why do we feel the need to give our children everything they ask for?

Fear of the Lord is the beginning of knowledge (Proverbs 1:7) and spurs on understanding, insight, and wisdom. A reverent respect for our Father brings us into His glory. If you and I cannot instill a heart of respect in our children for us, and for other adults, then how can we teach them to fear their heavenly Father?

In our current world, when our children radically love God and other people they will stand out. We as parents will be weirdos, completely off-kilter, misunderstood, undermined by other adults, even some in the church. Our children's peers will tell our kids how wrong and mean we are. Teachers and other parents will say we are closed-minded, judgmental, and prejudiced. But these better be said for the right reasons, and not because we are being idiots on our own tirades.

A radical lifestyle as a parent is not about us. When God chose to make us parents, he gave us an enormous responsibility. We will be held accountable! Our children are His children; they are Christ's bride and we need to view them that way. They are not ours to do with as we please. On the contrary, Jesus makes it clear that He loves children so much. If we lead his children, our kids, into sin; if we allow the world to disciple our children, then it would be better for you and I to have a gigantic rock tied around our necks and then throw ourselves into the depths of the oceans (Matthew 18:6). Do you think Jesus takes our words and actions towards our children lightly?

Let me bring another perspective on this. The church, you and I, are the bride of Christ. We can agree He loves all of us so much! Jesus says in Matthew 18:3-4 we must become like children to enter the kingdom of heaven. To see the bride as Jesus does is not to see the old man that is dead and gone, but to see the new creation (2 Corinthians 5:17) that lives in Christ (Galatians 2:20).

Jesus sees His beautiful bride, as they truly are, that is, dead to sin and alive to Christ (Romans 6:11). He sees the greatness of who He created us to be and who we are becoming. He sees the gifts in us. He sees us with the upgrades He has planned for us. He looks at us with unconditional love. He is unrelenting in pouring out blessings over us to complete fullness. To the point that we cannot help but display what He is doing in each of us. Therefore, it not only elicits uncontrollable praise and delight in God, but it experientially teaches us a truth that changes our very personalities and characters.

When God sees something missing in his children, he does NOT see the sin, because he already dealt with sin in Jesus. Instead, he sees where righteousness is lacking in that area of our lives. He teaches us and loves us not simply with words, but with actions and truth (1 John 3:18). God does not just tell us about peace, for example, when we worry and are anxious. He allows circumstances in our lives that create worry and anxiety when we focus on them. Then as we refocus on the Holy Spirit, He pours out peace and rest. When we experience Jesus's peace that supersedes our own understanding and guards our hearts and minds (Philippians 4:7) from the troubles in our circumstances, then we have just experienced a miracle.

God just dealt with our righteousness, and through experience, the peace of God becomes a tangible truth in our lives. Something that is true becomes truth when we experience it. If we know about kindness, but we do not live in kindness and we do not act in kindness towards others, then what good is it to know about kindness? Our Father teaches us kindness by speaking kindness into our lives and showering acts of kindness over us.

Jesus takes very seriously our leading our children to Him, or to the world. They will either have a friendship with the world and hate God (James 4:4) or they will be rejected and hated by the world and live an abundant life in Christ (John 10:10). Our children will live radical lives. There is no middle ground. If we love or teach our children to love the world or anything in it, then the love of the Father is not in us, or our children (1 John 2:15).

Moses, after he and God had a conversation on some new policies, told Israel that God is calling them to live radical lives. God tells him, "Mo, you've got to help these people, but they've got to obey, they've got to fear me, so they can all enjoy a long life in this beautiful land I've got for them (paraphrased)." Here is what everyone must do!

"Love the Lord your God with all your heart and with all your soul, and with all your strength. These commands I give you today are to be upon your hearts. Impress them on your children. Talk about them when you sit at home and when you walk along the road, when you lie down, and when you get up. Tie them as symbols on your hands and bind them on your foreheads. Write them on the door frames of your houses and on your gates" (Deuteronomy 6:4-9).

Be infatuated with me, obsessed with me. Because I am infatuated with each of you. I am utterly obsessed with loving every one of you and pouring more blessings and favor over you than you could ever ask or imagine. I love everything about you, so I have let you in on this secret about how to unlock this door to my glory. I want you to experience me in a way that you want nothing more than to teach your children about how great I Am.

Teach them about me when they get up in the morning, because I want to bless your family right off the bat each day. Then when you're driving around, to all the unnecessary activities you feel are crucial to your child's social and physical success, use that time to worship me and teach your kids how to delight in me. Impress these commands, my Word, on your children when they mess up, when they cry, whine, disobey, fight, succeed, obey, share, display love and kindness, etc. Make these teachable moments. Be late to practice so you can pull over when the children disobey and teach them how important obedience is to God.

In John 14:21 Jesus says that whoever loves me obeys my commands. Apart from all the other obvious reasons we obey, we show Jesus and our heavenly Father we love them. It is a way that our children display their love for God and their honor and love for us as their parents.

Then He also says to talk about Him, God, when we sit at home. Whatever God is highlighting in your lives find a way to make it applicable to your family and have a devotional, a mini-church in your home. That just shut some of you down right there, didn't it? Put you right over the edge, huh?

Make an event out of bedtime some nights. Bring God into their hearts and minds before they lay down. Teach them to pray, maybe the Lord's Prayer, maybe one that correlates with what they are learning on Sunday mornings. Intertwine God with their day as they tell you about it. Create and use teachable moments.

What is the glaring elephant in the room with all of this? You and I as parents must be in obedience in our heavenly lives. We must be living radically different from those around us at work, in our activities, schools, and even church sometimes. God created you and me to live abundant lives in Christ. Lives where instead of complaining we bless people, instead of being angry we learn and live out gentleness and patience. Instead of hating our enemies, we send them anonymous letters of encouragement.

When we point out the treasure in others, then that is what will come out, that is what we'll see. But, if we point out the faults, the sins, the mistakes and bad choices, and the dead man in people and our children, then that is what will come to the surface. We reap what we sow (Gal 6:7). Sow encouragement, blessings, prayer, love, mercy, kindness, and you will reap these in your own life and bring new life to your children and those around you. God will shower, no flood you with these, why? Because you and I reap what we sow!

A radical life for a child begins with a radical life lived by their parents. Our children, when they see and experience the love and grace of God in their lives, through you and I as their parents, will live radically different. They will learn to love God and delight in Him, to run in the freedom of His commands (Psalm 119:32). They will see Jesus in those they meet and pour out love on their enemies.

We are molding the next generation. We are leaving a legacy for our children. A legacy of what? What legacy will we leave for our children and grandchildren?

9

CALL TO ACTION

As a warrior remains in constant training with a focus on the enemy, driving him to push harder, through blood, sweat, and tears, he knows when the battles come every fight is life or death. He has a single focus: train and prepare for war to protect his family, his people, and his kingdom. His passion and focus is undivided. He lives for one purpose … to serve the King. His life revolves around this purpose and everything he does somehow relates back to his calling as a warrior.

He is in constant training, but that is never the goal or the end-state. It is preparation for his purpose. Every moment he is looking for a fight, an opportunity to push back the enemy and advance the kingdom. He is never content in the training because a burning desire within him cries out for more.

His intentionality in the pursuit of war inspires the other warriors and drives away their fears. He loves to serve the King and feels the most alive in the midst of battle beckoning the dawn of a new level of freedom for his people. He does not wait for others to volunteer or agree with what he knows his King is calling him to do. He can't wait. An urgency runs through his blood because he knows the enemy is angry and has a single focus on the destruction of the people. He cannot stand idly by and neither can we.

Be sober-minded; be watchful. Your adversary the devil prowls around like a roaring lion, seeking someone to devour (1 Peter 5:8). He has come to steal, kill, and destroy (John 10:10). He takes no captives and shows no mercy. This is not a game or to be taken lightly. Woe to you, O earth and sea, for the devil has come down to you in great wrath because he knows that his time is short (Revelation 12:12)!

The devil is not delayed by worrying about what people think or ensuring he understands and agrees with every principle or belief. His focus is destruction by any means available. Why are we hesitant to move, to declare our battle cry, break the mold and charge forward? Why do we not fight with every possible weapon? For though we walk in the flesh, we do not wage war against the flesh. For the weapons of our warfare are not of the flesh but have divine power to destroy strongholds (2 Corinthians 10:3-4).

We cannot delay, yet we waste time and lose momentum wondering if people will misinterpret what we feel that we should say or do. We fear what our fellow warriors will think or if they will reject us if it is ineffective. We are too timid to act on promptings and falsely believe we need to continue to study to increase knowledge before we step on the battlefield.

Where do we learn the greatest lessons? Which warriors are chosen to lead others? Is it not those who have thrown caution to the wind? Those who have recklessly abandoned their status or personal safety, and charged forward? Is it not those who have the scars from painful lessons through experience?

Do you want to fight next to someone who has studied war for decades in the confines of a library or a warrior who has been in the fight, learned through experience, and provides knowledge through perception received in the midst of chaos?

The reason the Son of God appeared was to destroy the works of the devil. (1 John 3:8b) Jesus laid down His life for us and we ought to lay down our lives for others. This life is not about us. It is about loving God and loving others through the grace and power of the Holy Spirit. There is no fear in love, but perfect love casts out fear (1 John 4:18).

We do not run aimlessly; we do not box as one beating the air. But we discipline our bodies and keep them under control (1 Corinthians 9:26)! We have a choice in every circumstance. We can stand idly by as the enemy ravishes our families and cities, which is the safe and easy answer that allows us more time to figure things out. Or ... we can ...

Let love be genuine. Abhor, that is to hate with a passion, what is evil and hold fast to what is good. We can outdo one another in showing honor, forsaking laziness but being fervent in the spirit, serving the Lord (Romans 12:9-11).

O you, who love the Lord, hate evil (Psalm 97:10)!

What if our hatred for evil and love for Jesus superseded every other thought, doubt, and fear we have that keeps us from recklessly abandoning all else in our pursuit of advancing the kingdom of heaven.

Therefore, since we are surrounded by so great a cloud of witnesses, let us also lay aside every weight and sin which clings so closely, and let us run with endurance the race that is set before us, looking to Jesus the founder and perfecter of our faith ... (Hebrews 12:1-2).

10

CONTENTMENT

We will never find contentment in what we do. The abundant life we seek is not in our activities. It's not in our hobbies, work, family, or friends. It's' not in the daily activities or the special activities we plan and look forward to. These will not give the contentment we seek. They may, at best, give a temporary fix, a small escape from our depravity, but they will always pass away and there will never be enough of them. We will always seek more.

There will come times when we sit and think about what we want to do, what sounds good, what would be fun, what would fill the void right now? And there is nothing that comes to mind. We rack our brains to strive for something that will give us a temporary escape from the dullness and discontentment we feel. So we lazily go to what will numb us or allow our minds to forget the troubles. We go to drugs or alcohol, sexual activities, movies or TV, social media, working out, shopping, or extreme sports. Anything to take our mind off of the stress and give us a moment of reprieve.

We desire to escape. We make the cowardly, easy, lazy choice … why? Because we instinctively want to gratify the desires of our sinful nature. It is the path of least resistance. After all, we are tired, work hard, and deserve it right? It's not about the activities. It's about the discontentment. It's about you and me clinging to our worries and our stresses. Holding onto the 'woe is me' story and making excuses for our thoughts and behaviors.

Were we created for ourselves? Were you and I created by the God of the universe to live self-indulgent, self-seeking lives? Contentment comes when we live and breathe the way we were created to live and breathe. Our spirits awaken when we lift our eyes to heaven and speak praises to our God. When we take the thoughts and problems of our lives, the things that drive us to false contentment, and lay them down at the feet of Jesus, surrender them and submit them, then we find rest and a peace that transcends all understanding and guards our hearts and minds in Christ Jesus (Philippians 4:7).

This is not always easy. Sometimes this takes blood, sweat, and tears. Sometimes it takes everything we have to fight and push and not give in to our flesh or the enemy. The road is narrow, my friends. The path is not easily found. Contentment throughout every moment of every day is found in Christ alone. Ask Him for it. Ask to be content in Him. Pursue Him for peace and joy in Him and not in some activity or material item.

Enjoy the activities or the things He gives us because He is doing them with us. Because He gave them to us. Let His words never depart from our mouths, but meditate on them day and night (Joshua 1:6). Write them on your hearts (Proverbs 7:3). We find fulfillment when we grow in our relationship with our Father. When we grant Him the time to speak love and grace and mercy into our hearts and minds.

We cannot love the world or the things of the world and truly love God (1 John 2:15). The things which we seek to fill our void is what we place our faith and trust in. The things which we seek out for pleasure, to give us an escape from reality, are taking the place of God. God came to bring us life abundantly (John 10:10).

The joy of the Lord is our strength (Neh. 8:10). Take joy in His creations, but He receives the glory. Rejoice in the gifts He gives, all for His glory.

Contentment must be found in Him. We were created to bring glory to God, to know Him, and to love Him. What or who we place our comfort, security, retreat, our escape in … that is our God. Where your treasure is, there your heart will be (Matthew 6:21). God wants to be our everything! To find true contentment in anything but Him is to believe a lie and take from our creator what He has given us and created us for.

Before we pray and focus on circumstances we first must pray and focus on Jesus.

LOOK TO JESUS BEFORE LOOKING TO CIRCUMSTANCES.

11

DEPENDENCE

The Lord is establishing and building in you a dependence on Him and others. Dependence is difficult to accept because it can be viewed as a weakness, or an inability to succeed or accomplish a task or mission. We were created to be dependent and strength comes through acknowledgment of weakness, resulting in dependence.

This process can lead to two conditions. The first condition is a resistance to developing dependence, resulting in the build-up of walls to mask emotions and perceived signs of weakness. This creates a hard heart attempting self-protection from vulnerability and emotional responses. This is counter-productive to the development of dependence on the Spirit and on others.

The second condition is the belief in, and subsequent obedience to, Jesus's words to Paul. "My grace (that is, his empowering presence) is sufficient for you, for my power is made perfect in your weakness." Paul then states he will boast all the more gladly about his weaknesses so that the power of Christ may rest upon him (2 Corinthians 12:9).

Dependence requires a reckless abandonment of self-preservation and letting go of characteristics about ourselves we hold dear. It is letting our strength and security come from Jesus so our hearts remain tender and we draw life from His Living Water (John 7:38-39).

Resistance to dependence creates walls, hardens the heart, isolates, and diminishes our fruit of the Spirit and open, honest communion with Jesus. We are saying, "You are not enough, you cannot handle this, I need to take care of it myself, in a way that I know, understand, and that feels safer to me. But I love you and trust you, Jesus." Well … no we do not trust Him when we think and respond like this.

Dependence is the ultimate vulnerability. It is conceding to open our hearts wide and say, "Lord, I am weak, you are strong. I feel like I will get my heart broken with it unprotected like this. I feel like I have no control, which is very scary, and I do not know how to be strong and deal with issues and hold myself together like this. Please be gentle with me and my heart because I am, in faith and trust, releasing it to you, refusing to build walls and harden my heart for protection. I want to remain sensitive to you, and kind and compassionate to those around me. Flood me now with your peace that guards my heart and mind in Christ Jesus."

Thank you, Lord.

12

DISCIPLINE: ESAU

"Endure hardship as discipline; God is treating you as sons" (Hebrews 12:7).

---

iscipline and focus are essential elements to a life of following Christ. We must train in the physical, but more so in the spiritual, where all good gifts come from (1Timothy 4:8, James 1:17).

This is crucial. When we have a desire, outside of Christ, that we allow to consume us, because of a lack of discipline and focus on the eternal, we may lose something of great importance. In the blink of an eye we could find ourselves off the narrow road, in a ditch, outside of God's will, or destroying our own destiny the Father has planned, along with the relationships of those around us.

Esau, for a single meal, sold/gave up his rightful inheritance as a son. God had inheritance and promises for Esau that he never received because He gratified the desire of His sinful nature (Galatians 5:16). He lost focus of the eternal, of what is truly important. His lack of self-discipline, which comes from a life of obedience to our Lord, cost him so much. One compromise, one thought or word or action is all it takes for us to choose our will instead of the Father's will.

Duet. 30:19-20a says, "This day I call heaven and earth as witnesses against you that I have set before you life and death, blessings and curses. Now choose life, so that you and your children may live and that you may love the Lord your God, listen to His voice, and hold fast to Him. For the Lord is your Life …

In Deuteronomy 31:6 we read, "Be strong and courageous. Do not be afraid or terrified because of them, for the Lord your God goes with you; He will never leave you nor forsake you."

13

EMOTIONS

Many sins are sins of emotion. Feelings that arise from our flesh that you and I allow to dictate our thoughts and actions. For the Spirit is willing but the body is weak (Matthew 26:4). A deep longing inherent in the sinful nature of each of us, coupled with societal norms and pressures, leave us constantly satisfying our fleshly, sinful desires.

Someone is rude, we become offended, we act, or at least think, based on our emotions. We see something we want, whether it is a person, place, or thing, and it is our emotions that begin to feed either our fleshly sinful desires or our spirit. When we choose to walk in the Spirit, we will not gratify the desires of our sinful nature (Galatians 5:16).

So then, the antecedent, the antidote, the reversal agent for our sins birthed from emotion is peace. A heart and mind controlled by the Spirit is life and peace (Romans 8:6). But those controlled by the sinful nature cannot please God (Romans 8:8). A heart and mind at peace do not become overwhelmed by fleshly emotions that lead us into thoughts and actions drawing us out of God's presence. For this is love for God: to obey His commands (1 John 5:3).

In fact, Jesus has given each of us as His children a special gift. When Jesus told His disciples about the coming of the Holy Spirit, He left them with peace. Not just any peace, but 'my peace I give you' (Matthew 14:27). Paul brings this wonderful peace up again. The peace of God, which transcends all understanding, will guard our hearts and minds in Christ Jesus (Philippians 4:7). He has left this with us. In this peace, Jesus tells us not to have a troubled heart or to be afraid (John 14:27). His peace applies to and combats both of these.

Troubled hearts and fear generally manifest themselves as emotions which in turn lead us to think and act in our flesh (Romans 8:5). Jesus offers rest for the weary (Matthew 11:29-30). He will take any and all troubles, worries, fears, and burdens from those who come to Him, lay them down in humility and submission, and then accept His yoke and burden (Matthew 11:29-30).

Jesus's response is to give us rest, peace, gentleness, and humility. You WILL find rest. We live in a peace that the world cannot comprehend or even begin to fathom, and it literally guards our hearts, the wellspring of life (Proverbs 4:23), and our minds (Philippians 4:7). A mind submitted to the Spirit is life and peace. It's not a characteristic of this mind, it is the substance of it (Romans 8:6).

To have peace is to have a stability of the heart and mind that is surrendered to Christ, controlled by the Spirit, and therefore uninfluenced by the world, the devil, or the flesh. Peace is to take a deep breath and breathe in the breath of the Almighty. Feeling His peace flow through your body, filling it from the inside out. Then exhaling and blowing out, releasing whatever circumstances around you and in you that are troubling your heart and/or creating fear, the stress, negative emotions, and doubt. They're gone ... let them go (Matthew 6:33-34).

14

EMOTIONS: WHY OUR HEARTS MUST BE YIELDED

G od has given us a new heart that is alive and well. This does not mean it is perfect, that we can always listen to it, or that it is ours to do with as we please. It must be yielded to Him, consecrated to Him, set apart as something sacred, very sacred, to be devoted wholly to God, for His purposes. Our hearts are precious and must be protected. Emotions: love, joy, sadness, envy, pride, anger, fear, resentment, lust, judgment. These come from the heart. If our hearts are not yielded to God, then we cannot produce His fruit.

We cannot control our hearts, just as we alone cannot control our tongues. Data enters through the senses he has given us, they enter through our brain, so right there, every thought must be taken captive to be made obedient to Christ (2 Corinthians 10:5) and I must beat my body and make it my slave so that after I have preached to others I myself will not be disqualified for the prize (1 Corinthians 9:27).

We are not at liberty to flippantly act on impulse, allowing our flesh to dictate our thoughts and hearts. This will destroy others, especially those we love, and separate us from the presence of God. We must be quick to listen, slow to speak, and slow to become angry (James 1:19).

For our hearts to maintain control of our emotions by means of the Holy Spirit, it must be yielded to our sovereign, loving, grace-filled Father. Then, and only then, will we be a useful servant to our master. If our character is not developed how are we to be sent out by Him, for Him? Does an athlete not have to condition his body before the race? So we must be conditioned as well. Consecrated and yielded to Christ so that He may awaken our souls and breathe His breath of life into us. Remember faith, hope, and love ... but the greatest of these is love (1 Corinthians 13:13).

15

EXALTATION FOR GLORIFICATION

To the humble, He gives grace (Proverbs 3:34). Jesus says that the humble will be exalted (Matthew 23:12).

James reminds the believers that whoever humbles himself before the Lord will be exalted by God himself (James 4:10) and given more grace (James 4:6), His empowering presence.

Peter declares and mandates to humble ourselves under the mighty hand of God so that at the proper time we might be exalted (1 Peter 5:6).

When we think, talk, and act in humility, it is a reflection of the acknowledgment of our proper place before God. Humility is knowing, from our heart, our rightful place before the Almighty King, on our knees at his feet.

Humility is not thinking less of ourselves but seeing more of God. Humility is not belittling of us or refusing appreciation from others. Humility is having such an enormous and awe-inspiring view of God that we gladly accept thanks and appreciation because we know it is the work of God in us, either directly or through the gifts, time, and talents he has bestowed upon us.

When Father sees our excitement in Him, especially when others recognize His work in us, He is thrilled to receive His rightful glory and worship, both from us giving thanks for His work in us and others seeing His work and acknowledging He is Lord.

One who will not accept good things or thanks for appreciation from others may be attempting humility, but they are actually bound in a form of pride that acts as false humility. This person rejects praise because they are thinking it is for them because of their own greatness.

In pride, they are taking ownership and the glory of the successful actions and corresponding kind words. A humble heart gladly accepts honors given because everything in their life points to Jesus. They know, even if it cannot always be verbalized, that those present will have to acknowledge God in the success. Why?

Because a life of humility must consistently and constantly point to the Creator. It is a life lived in daily dependence on and worship of Him.

So you see, when the humble man, whose life is a reflection of Jesus, is appreciated by others, His first thought is gratitude and worship to God. He is excited at God's great work in His life again, whether directly or through time, talents, or tithes. There is no ownership so there is no need for the "it's not me, woe is me, etc." God is glorified through a life dedicated to Him. Jesus prayed to be glorified so the Father might be glorified (John 17:1).

Our initial thought should not be how do I deflect this appreciation because the root of that is false humility grown in pride. The first thought is the heart's cry "thank you, Lord, you are so awesome, let your name be glorified in this. Let it never be me, to your glory, let it be you completely."

This is the heart's cry between us and the Lord. What is spoken reflects gratitude and excitement and, if proper and fitting, a verbal recognition of God's great mercy and grace at work.

The point is that this last statement may not always be necessary because our lives should have already spoken these words.

God loves to exalt the humble man because He is certain by His lifestyle and overflowing heart of gratitude in recognition of God's very breath in him, that He will be glorified. The world will come to know He is Lord through the exaltation of the humble man because exalting a humble heart will glorify the Father.

16

FOR THE SAKE OF
THE WORLD

ove, grace, gratitude, humility, brokenness, weakness.
These form the character that God has recruited us to live
out. A character of meekness. Controlled strength. A true,
clear view of our own insufficiency driving us to a brokenness and
dependence on our Father. "What we are not in ourselves is used
by God to bring blessings to others." (Graham Cooke, Spiritual
Warrior, p. 121) Not to bring glory to ourselves. Not to make
us feel more adequate, useful, or productive, but for the sake of
the world (1 Thessalonians 2:19-20 - you are our glory and joy).

"We live with God in our weakness, and we live in Him
because of the power that other people need to have directed
at them through our lifestyle" (Graham Cooke, Spiritual
Warrior, 121).

How glorious is it that none of this is about you or me. We do
nothing for ourselves and we can do nothing by ourselves (John
15:5). This is the glorious freedom we have been given by our
Lord. God works in and through us for the sake of the world.
God has a plan, go and reach the nations, and he uses the lowly

and humble of the world as a conduit for his amazing grace and power to awe the world. To bring them to their knees. That every tongue will confess Jesus Christ is Lord. Take joy and be glad, stay humble, live in meekness so that you are a fire hydrant poured into from an endless source and therefore an eternal outpouring.

You and I need to be in a state of meekness for people to see Christ in us. They need His love and grace. They need His power. These are not simply wants or desires, they are desperate needs; even though some of them, some of us, don't know that yet. God's chosen us, so we need to obey … for the sake of the world. We may be God's only plan to bring Christ's light to the dark world around us.

17

GOD'S WILL

God's will for us is in our heart, our mind, our soul, our character, NOT in our actions. Not in what we do. God's will for us is NOT, primarily, to do all of these things you and I strive to do. God's will is a reflection of His beloved Son Jesus in you and me. Our Father's will is for us to love always. To love our enemies and friends alike. To display meekness and humility in the depths of our hearts.

God's will is for us to trust and believe in him like a child. To not make assumptions, but to always be open to the impossible, to dream of the beautiful, and expect the extraordinary. God's will for you and me is to be so enamored with him that it appears we are disinterested in everything else if it weren't for the compassion, mercy, and care that floods from our hearts out to those in need.

Our 'being' like Jesus must be our Father's will on earth as it is in heaven because apart from Him we can do nothing (John 15:5).

We must fall to the ground and die as a seed (John 12:24). We must live out our lives not in what we do or accomplish, but as a lover. A lover of Jesus, of God our Father, of the Holy Spirit, and of the people we encounter along the path our Father has planned for us. We must live our lives 'being' as Jesus was so that we might DO as Jesus did. That is, what He saw His Father doing and speaking what His Father spoke. Lowering Himself in obedience to poverty, to servanthood, to ridicule, to torture, to be a curse (Galatians 3:13), to death, to separation from the presence of His Father.

WITHOUT BEING WHO HE WAS, HE NEVER COULD HAVE DONE WHAT HE DID!

18

GROWING PAINS

When growth takes place there is a stretching, tearing, breaking down, and a rebuilding, expanding process that takes place.

When this process is slow and gradual the results are not as evident at a glance. To see them the growth process must be constantly monitored and then viewed over time. This manner of growth is rarely painful because of the minute changes taking place day by day. But solid, stable results happen through slow and gradual growth. Slow growth can be frustrating because of the time it takes, but it is a more peaceful and gentle process.

Fast growth, on the other hand, can be violent, jolting, and take time to mature into. During times of rapid growth there is pain because of the accelerated process of tearing, breaking down, and rebuilding that takes place. Rapid growth can be exciting as results and progress are seen immediately; while simultaneously it can be dreadful because of the pain, discomfort, and confusion that will inevitably accompany it.

We are learning to walk in the newness of life. Putting off the old self, being renewed in the spirit of our minds, putting on the new self, created after the likeness of God in true righteousness and holiness (Ephesians 4:22-24).

At any time, as we learn to walk in newness of life, we are growing according to Christ's gifts of grace, plans, and purposes for our lives. Certain areas of our lives will have seasons of rapid growth, and others slow, steady growth. We must always know that the lovingkindness of the Father is to make us more like Him, growing us in maturity and love and grace, according to His power at work within us.

19

A PRAYER

Good morning Father, Jesus, Holy Spirit. Today I want to follow you. I deny pride; please grant me humility; I deny anger - grant me patience and compassion; I deny selfishness - fill me with a servant's heart; I deny lust - give me a respect for women, and a fresh attractiveness for my spouse.

I take up my cross today. I recognize and remember your sacrifice on the cross and how you died once for all. You died as me on the cross. When I accepted your gift my flesh died when you died and I became born again (John 3). I am a new creation in Christ, pure, being made in your righteousness.

I keep the old man dead by declaring my abundant life in Jesus. Having been born again I am new and no longer a slave to sin, death, or the world. As I take up my cross, I focus on the life-giving work of Jesus and the truth that as I abide in Christ as His beloved son, my old man stays dead.

I follow you today, Lord Jesus. I follow you to abandon all else. It is to take a narrow path isolating me from the path the world is on. Following you is knowing your voice, your mind, your heart, and your will. Reveal these to me today. Teach me to hear and know your voice more because I am your sheep. Fill me with your presence as I tread on your heels.

Following you requires my unquestionable obedience. I will obey you today Father no matter the order. No matter the sacrifice, or how illogical it sounds, or how silly or weird I feel. You are my life, my everything. I live to follow you. Every part of my life is dedicated to serving, loving, and worshipping you. Today I abide in you, I deny myself, take up my cross, and follow you (Luke 9:23).

20

THE AUTHORITY BEHIND IT ...

Matthew 7:28b-29 says "...The crowds were amazed at His teaching because He taught as one who had authority."

Sometimes it is not what we say that influences others as much as the source and the authority behind it.

Authority is not something a person can conjure up. It is a right given by one with the position to grant it.

Jesus spoke with authority because His teaching was not His own, it came from the Father (John 7:16-17), so the words were spirit and life (John 6:63). Jesus did not do His own will, but the will of the Father (John 6:38). He did nothing on His own but spoke just what the Father taught Him (John 8:28).

Jesus spoke and moved with authority because He had received His identity from His Father (Luke 3:22) and was full of the Holy Spirit (Luke 4:1). No miracle or ministry is in the Bible before He received these. So through surrender and submission of His own will to the Father, He was filled with the Holy Spirit, assured of who He was in His Father's eyes and He knew His promises and inheritance (Luke 4:18, 2 Peter 1:3-4).

As Jesus was in this world so we are like Him (1 John 4:17). We are one with Him (Galatians 3:28, 1 Corinthians 6:17) and alive to God in Christ Jesus (Romans 6:10). He sent us out with the authority to trample on snakes and scorpions and the authority to overcome all the power of the enemy (Luke 10:19). We have authority from the one whom all were created by and all things were created for (Colossians 1:16) ... Jesus Christ.

The people, after the most awesome sermon was given, were amazed and moved by His authority, not like that of the Pharisee teachers. He didn't solely read the Bible, repeating law, He spoke with unction from the Holy Spirit, the perspective, the massive lens change that the Father gave Him.

You have heard, but now I say ... He brought a new, beautiful, heavenly perspective that was describing the new covenant which was in transition from the old at that very moment. We also are given authority where God has put us: in our families, our places of influence (work, hobbies), etc. We are given responsibility and with it the authority to affect eternal change through the power of Jesus Christ.

21

BADGES, HONOR,
AND GLORY

Each day brings an opportunity to store up badges, honors, and glory for the earth, the temporal; or it allows us to bring glory to Jesus, change the lives of those around us for the rest of eternity, and store up treasures and honor for ourselves in heaven that will last for eternity.

Each day is about me or it's about God. Every word, thought, action and decision are either focused on the temporal or it is focused on the eternal. I'm investing in my own glory, how people see me here on earth, or I am bringing glory to the Almighty King, disregarding myself and what people will think of me for this short temporary time on earth.

This time is preparation for our everlasting eternity worshipping and dancing in the presence of the Most High God!

22

COMMUNICATION
WITH HONOR

We as men, are intentionally, and sometimes unintentionally, brought up to keep our feelings, emotions, and annoyances to ourselves. We are told it is women who openly discuss what's going through their head or minor offenses they have taken from a friend or co-worker, whether real or perceived.

Yet miscommunication and/or lack of communication will kill an otherwise healthy, honoring environment. Satan jumps on the opportunity to throw fuel on the fire of a small offense, again, actual or perceived, by one of the parties. He bombards us with thoughts of negativity and division. He wants to remove the benefit of the doubt we would give. He loathes a loving mindset that sees, thinks, and expects the best in those around us and refuses to constantly be offended. Satan wants to magnify our insecurities and fears that cause us to be offended.

In a culture of communication with honor, we find the freedom to be who we are in Christ without fear of condemnation or judgment. We can speak openly and honestly with each other because we know that the man across from us is seeing through the lens of Jesus, with grace, mercy, and love. It means he acknowledges the positional authority we have in Christ and our role in the kingdom of heaven.

When we find ourselves in conflict, because we live, move, and speak in freedom, we take a moment to find the root of it. We then take it to the person, not with accusations, but with a description of our perception of the situation. It's safe without accusation and the knowledge that relationship is more important than the conflict.

Most conflicts stem from fear and insecurity. For us to know that, above all else, both parties are protecting the relationship with each other, and even more so each other's relationships with Christ, will put at ease the defensiveness that births from the common beliefs we must defend and protect ourselves. This is the case in a culture of honor as we place Christ at the center as the common ground of what heaven is doing in, around, and through us (our mission); and then unity; followed by the interests of others; and finally our own interests and desires.

Freedom is allowing people to live in their calling and helping to develop what God is doing in them, not what we want to develop in them.

A culture of communication with honor gives us peace that those around us are being genuine and we can trust and accept what they say. We can be sure that there is no facade because they would come to discuss the conflict or situation if communication or intent is not clear. For us to create and maintain this culture we must know and accept who we are in Christ and be totally committed to living out that identity as sons of the Most High God.

We must treat each other according to the names given to us by our Father, not aliases we have received from the world. And finally, we must live and work from a place acknowledging the interdependence in the skills, roles, gifts, experience, and anointing God has distributed and their design functioning as a team, creating a 'funnel' from heaven to earth.

In this culture, we will honor God, flourish in unity, and see heaven open. We will be a part of the supernatural work God is doing in the spiritual realm around us, eternally impacting the kingdom of heaven.

23

DEMONIC INFLUENCE

emonic influence is like an older friend or playmate when one is a child. They can plant ideas and influence a younger playmate without them really knowing what is going on until they find themselves wondering how they got into the situation they are in or why they did what they did. They don't see it for what it is until they get in trouble and someone (usually the parent) points out what they did. Bad company corrupts good character (1 Corinthians 15:13).

Satan is the father of lies; that is his native tongue. He came to steal, kill, and destroy. He hates those who follow Christ and the greatest weapon he has is to persuade believers that he doesn't exist, or that he doesn't influence or bother them. If he can make followers of Christ believe that every negative thought and feeling, word, and action is birthed and grown in their own mind and heart then he is not seen as a threat. Therefore he is ignored, and they accept and heap all of the guilt and shame on themselves. Believing there is no outside influence, there is never authority taken over it and the enemy is never combated.

It's like they have leeches and ticks all over their back, sucking the blood and life out of them. Refusing to grasp there is an external source to their weakness and sickness they simply try harder and get more frustrated with themselves because it is believed that they are getting weaker of their own accord. They ... we ... feel guilty and shameful when we don't act or think or speak in the way we want to or know we should. It's all our fault.

We are always responsible for our thoughts and actions. But it is naive and very dangerous to dismiss the devil's role and influence in this world. Without recognition of the source of the mindset or the flowing stream of thoughts or actions, it cannot be shut down.

We can't kill what we don't know exists. We can't kill what we don't see and believe is a threat to us. We'll never target what we don't perceive as a threat.

"Be self-controlled and alert. Your enemy the devil prowls around like a roaring lion looking for someone to devour. Resist him, standing firm in the faith ... and Christ ... will Himself restore you and make you strong, firm, and steadfast" (1 Peter 5:8,9a,10b).

"But woe to the earth and the sea, because the devil has gone down to you! He is filled with fury because he knows that his time is short" (Revelation 12:12b).

We face an enemy that is dedicated above all else to their cause, to the devil, to the destruction of anyone who attempts to follow Christ. He is focused and has thousands of years of experience. He has an army composed of foot soldiers and then specialists.

Specialists are spirits that focus on specific sin: a spirit of lust, of lies, of anger, bitterness, confusion, unforgiveness, insecurity, pride, masturbation, etc. They are trained in these through the study of our behaviors and how we operate. This is war, real war.

"For though we live in the world, we do not wage war as the world does. The weapons we fight with are not the weapons of the world. On the contrary, they have divine powers to demolish strongholds. We demolish arguments and every pretension that sets itself up against the knowledge of God, and we take captive every thought to make it obedient to Christ" (2 Corinthians 10:3-5).

We are in a war and the enemy finds soft targets and demolishes them. The enemy has limited resources and time so he must choose who he focuses on. We must live in such a way that we are a waste of time, effort, and resources to the enemy because he has no effect on us. Because we train our spirit, mind, and body in obedience to the King of Kings.

24

EVERY DESIRE

Every desire we have has its roots in a desire for the Lord. He created all things. We have voids of contentment or pleasure that we seek to fulfill with sexuality, adventure, acceptance, control, food, gifts and presents, or power. The abundant life we are offered is not fulfilled or attained through any of these. Our contentment will never be satisfied with these, but only with an increase of Jesus in our lives. All we seek has its roots in the Lord Almighty. Only he can indulge and satisfy every passion and desire that burns within us.

Father, what is it that I am seeking in you when I am led to believe (by the flesh or devil) that I want …?

"My soul will be satisfied as with the richest foods; with singing lips, my mouth will praise you" (Psalm 63:5).

"I will refresh the weary and satisfy the faint" (Jeremiah 31:25).

There is an inherent 'doing' in finding satisfaction in anything other than the King.

"When I fed them, they were satisfied; when they were satisfied they became proud; then they forgot me" (Hosea 13:6).

We also become defensive of that which satisfies us; in our pride, we defend and justify and rationalize and validate to vindicate ourselves of any guilt or shame.

25

EXPECTATIONS

My son/daughter, release the expectations and the pressure. I am releasing you from them. Live by principle, not pressure. Live for love, not expectations of greatness through performance. I will give you and speak to you all that you need and desire at exactly the right time. Enjoy this time of observing, watching, and serving. Look at everyone through the lens of humility and love.

Yes, I will do so much through you and raise you up. You will be known in the kingdom of heaven, even here on earth. But that's not your concern or focus. You will always be under pressure and focused on the wrong things when that is your desire. All of what you feel you will have through a love and excitement for Me and Me alone.

Yes, I have great plans for you and your family. But I bring it in my time when you are ready. Just stop! You are putting so much pressure on your self - stop it! You know me and you know My heart. I love you so much. I will fulfill my words and promises in you.

26

FREEDOM IN STATUTES

Word: I will run in the way of your commandments for you have set my heart free (Psalm 119:32). We will always be slaves to something or someone. We are born into this world as slaves to sin. The Lord's commandments lead us into freedom and a relationship with Him.

"I have stored up your words in my heart that I might not sin against you" (Psalm 119:11). We find freedom from the bondage of sin in His statutes. The common misconception is that God's commands are to bind us, to restrict our actions to please Him. There is a lie that His laws just tell us what to do and rule over us and keep us from living an exciting, fun-filled life.

There is no truth in that. On the contrary, we find delight in His commandments, which we grow to love. We lift up our hands in worship for His commandments and meditate on His statutes (Psalms 119:47-48). Why?

Because His word is a lamp to our feet and light to our path (Psalm 119:105). His precepts give us life (Psalm 119:93). His promises, within His Word, bring us comfort and prevent iniquity's dominion over us.

We were created for an intimate love relationship with our heavenly Father, Jesus, and the Spirit. These relationships are always initiated and carried by the Trinity through their grace, their empowering presence that enables us to become the men/women they already see. His laws, precepts, commandments, are light to the path leading us into a deeper relationship with the Trinity.

His statutes set us free from the slavery of sin and guide us into the right relationship with the Father. Through obedience to His statutes, we transition from slaves to sin to slaves of righteousness.

But do not be misled! We must not seek the knowledge of the word and miss seeing Jesus standing in front of us. The statutes are never the end in themselves. We are called to meditate on His laws, write them on the tablets of our hearts, but that is never the end state.

See, His statutes, laws, precepts, spiritual disciplines, meditation, contemplation, etc., are all for naught if they do not lead us into a beautifully transforming love relationship with Jesus Christ. If they do not cause our hearts to cry out and burn in worship for our Lord then why obey? Apart from the life-changing power of the Holy Spirit through them, leading us into the majestic life of freedom in Christ, they are empty practices and disciplines.

We delight in His laws and precepts because through them, by His grace, we remain in Him, free from the dominion of sin over us. Living in the righteousness of His statutes we discover joy, peace, and comfort unmatched by anything this world has to offer.

God hates sin because it separates His children from Him. He abhors evil because it is detrimental to the intimacy He seeks with His sons and daughters. So we too must come to love His statutes, His presence, and our relationship with Him, so much that we also grow to hate sin and abhor evil.

Sin enslaves and inhibits communion. But the statutes of the Lord bring us into freedom and life in Jesus Christ.

27

GOD IS LOVE

"So we have come to know and to believe the love that God has for us. God is love, and whoever abides in love abides in God, and God abides in him. By this is love perfected (made complete) within us" (1 John 4:16-17a).

Love is made full, complete, in us through being in the presence of God.

Father gives us Himself, that is the greatest act He could do. He pours His love, Himself, into our hearts THROUGH the Holy Spirit who has been given to us (Romans 5:5).

He gives us more of Him through the Spirit. We are strengthened with power through His Spirit (Ephesians 3:16) so that Christ may dwell in our hearts (Ephesians 3:17). The Father's love, Himself, is poured into our hearts through the Holy Spirit and Christ dwells in our hearts by power through the Holy Spirit.

To know the Love of Christ requires the power of Christ in us, through love. Knowledge of the love of Christ, leading to the fullness of God, does not come through book knowledge but through perception. The power of the Holy Spirit, through experiences in conjunction with the meditation of His Word, leads to a revelation of how much the Father loves us. The revealing of His love, Himself, comes through relationship, abiding, and is an ever-filling, never-ending process leading us to the fullness of God (Ephesians 3:19).

God IS love, poured into our hearts, through the abiding in and power of the Holy Spirit. Christ dwells in our hearts, through faith, by the power of the Holy Spirit. The result of this is the indwelling presence of Jesus and the Holy Spirit. It's a love relationship in abiding with them leading us to experience and discover the amazing love the Father has for us.

This opens our hearts to comprehend, through revelation, the love of Christ, filling us with all the fullness of God. His love for us is the root of the inconceivable power at work within us that is able to do far more than we could ask or think, all for the glory of Christ Jesus (Ephesians 3:20).

God IS love, and He, that is love, is made complete through abiding in Him. Taking comfort in the shadow of His wings; walking hand in hand with the Spirit throughout the day; scheduling times to be with the Father, both in conversation and meditation. It is incorporating the Spirit in every decision, thought, and action. Openly sharing the varying emotions of life: fear, anger, depression, sorrow, joy, etc.

We were created for an intimate, abiding love relationship with Father, Jesus, and the Spirit. It is in a relationship the Father pours His love, Himself, into our hearts through the Spirit. He gives Himself and He IS love!

28

GOD'S PRESENCE

ome to me. Are you trying to please me or to know me? You must know me to please me. If anyone wishes to come after Me he must deny himself, take up His cross daily, and follow me (Luke 9:23). It's not about you, or knowledge, or what you can tell others. It's about Me, the submission, recognition, and love of Me. All else pales in comparison. So put away what detracts of the freeing of your mind. A mind controlled by the Spirit is life and peace (Rom. 8:6). Make no agenda other than this: thirst and hunger for Me, seek, and you will find, knock and the door will be opened to you (Luke 11:9).

What does it look like to live out the truth that I am His chosen son/daughter?

It's living in the freedom I have given you - freedom from fear, freedom from sin, freedom from death. I want you to live in confidence, not pride in yourself, but confidence in me, my promises, and in the words I have spoken to you. I am loving and merciful, I am slow to anger and have more patience than you could ever comprehend. I am your Father and have great plans for you (Jeremiah 29:11 or 13). I am not looking down on you waiting to punish or take away from you. That is not how you look over your children, so why would I look over my children that way when I AM LOVE?

Development of gifts and power comes from, not a conscious thought and love for others, but from a heart conditioned and given over to God so there is an unconscious thought of compassion and love for others.

It is pure and independent of our desires. It is in response to the yielding of our heart to God and His unfathomable, unconditional love filling us from the very core of our heart and soul. It then flows outward until there is an un-conscious, even subliminal love of God overflowing from every thought and action.

This love leads us to our longings, compassion, and love to be where He is working, not where we want to be. That's the difference. That is when our faith is increased because we see God move every day and that is because we love as He loves, and our hearts yearn for and break for what His heart yearns for and breaks for.

To the pre-Christian: (a prophetic word) you don't know Me but I know you and I love you. You will never be fully fulfilled in this life without me. The void that you feel can't be filled with your job, your wife, guns, gear, nothing. Only by the blood of my Son Jesus Christ can you truly live in this dying world. I sent Jesus to earth to set an example and then to die as a replacement for your sins. It was an act of love and sacrifice. I want you to be My son. Believe My words ... for they are true. Accept my gift ... My Son to take your place. Receive Me in your life ... My Holy Spirit to live in you. Surrender all ... for Me to lead and guide you.

The almost depressed feeling you have is of this world, looking and focusing on what is seen in your circumstances. Come to Me and I will give you peace, hope, love, and freedom. Freedom from the bonds of slavery, of what this world considers the great things of life. I came to give freedom for freedom's sake, not to enslave with rules and commands. My commands are to protect, to guide, and are a way to display your love for Me.

Above all guard your heart, which is what the enemy is attacking. Your spouse, and your (future) children, need you to be the man/woman I created you to be. To love your spouse the way you truly desire will only come through being filled with my love. I am love.

29

HIS GLORY

I n Exodus 34 Moses's face shown radiant when he was in the presence of God. More specifically it says when God spoke to him. When Moses went and the Lord spoke to him, Moses's face shown bright with God's glory (His goodness) and all the people knew when Moses had been with God. It was only when Moses lifted his veil that God's glory was shown.

In the same way, when we turn to the Lord our veil is lifted, and in His presence we radiate His light and goodness. Daily, by the hour and minute, with every situation and in every interaction, we have the opportunity to bring glory to God and show His glory to others. All that stands in our way is our negative thought patterns that pull our focus off of Jesus, the Eternal, and onto ourselves and our circumstances.

God is with us, always. We have the Holy Spirit living within us. We have access to the throne room. We can live an untroubled life that is distinguished by the presence of God in all that we say and do. That is His influence in every thought, word, and action; a constant abiding in Jesus, hearing and obeying God's voice which empowers us to live a radical life following Him.

30

HOLY

Purity is living as the person that Christ sees when He looks at us. It is living in our true identity. We have now been reconciled in Christ's body of flesh by His death, in order to present us holy and blameless and above reproach (free from accusation) before Him (in His sight) (Colossians 1:22). When our heavenly Father looks at us He sees nothing wrong with us. And by that will (the Father's will for Jesus on earth) we have been sanctified through the offering of the body of Jesus Christ once for all (Hebrews 10:10). We have been brought into true fellowship with God. This is how God sees us; this is His perspective of us.

The way our Father looks at us is meant to empower us. His grace is the empowering presence of God that enables us to become the people that He already sees when He looks at us.

31

IN THE MOMENT

I n the moment of fear, He calls us up to courage and boldness. In the moment of sorrow, He wraps us in His comfort. In the moment of success and victory, He raises us into His joy and celebration. In the moment of sin, He empowers us with His grace. In the moment of repentance, we find mercy and forgiveness.

In every moment, with our eyes fixed on Jesus, the God of hope fills us with all joy and peace in believing, so that by the power of the Holy Spirit, we may abound in hope (Romans 15:13). There is hope in every moment, but it is not always easily visible. If then, in this moment, we have been raised with Christ, seek the things that are above, set your mind on the things that are above, not on things here on earth (Colossians 3:1-2). To focus on the moment is to miss the purpose of the moment, the opportunity within each moment.

Within every moment is an opportunity to glorify God or indulge the flesh, respond in patience or react in anger, dwell in peace or reside in turmoil, love God and abhor evil or love the world and hate God. Every moment presents an occasion to see circumstances and the people through the lens of Jesus or through the lens of selfish desires to gratify the flesh.

We are God's chosen ones and called to live in the moment as such. We have a spirit, not of fear or timidity, but love, power, and self-discipline (2 Timothy 1:7). We walk, talk, and think as the King's holy and beloved with compassionate hearts, in kindness and humility bearing with one another. In the moment, if one has a complaint against another, we forgive each other, as the Lord has forgiven us (Colossians 3:12-13). In every moment we draw from the love the Father has poured into our hearts through the Holy Spirit so that above all else we may put on love, which binds everything together in perfect harmony (Colossians 3:14).

32

JOINED WITH CHRIST

To abide in Christ is to be joined with Him in one spirit. For two to become one requires the abandonment of former identities, actions, thoughts; the relinquishing of self-desires and self needs. We must let go of all of us in order to take on all of Him.

As a cup of water loses its properties when poured into the vast ocean (or more accurately gains new properties suited for new purposes) the ocean engulfs the water and gives it a new purpose. That's obvious, but if the water thought it was still freshwater and was meant for its previous purposes then it would limit itself by its mindset. The water already has new properties and purposes of the ocean, but it doesn't live in it, accept it, or experience the freedom and purpose that it has. It's trying to hold onto its former particles and composition, unconsciously hindering itself to a futile cause fighting a process that is inevitable.

When the fresh water is poured into the ocean, it mentally, emotionally, and spiritually must accept the new infinity that it has entered into, though completely overwhelming and impossible to understand. But if its own will is released, laid down, and its new life in the ocean, with its new properties, new freedoms, and purposes, is accepted, then it will be joined and able to fully embrace the majestic fullness of its new life.

What if you and I struggle against and fight our new, true identity and purpose in the fullness of Christ that He has poured over us? How does the way we see ourselves catapult us into all Truth or hold us back, robbing us of the intended freedom in Christ? How does our view of our Father make us feel? Does your view of the Father melt your heart, put a smile on your face, and send a rush of peace and joy and rest over you?

The way that Jesus looks at us and speaks to us is meant to empower us!

"God's love has been poured into our hearts through the Holy Spirit who has been given to us" (Romans 5:5b).

We either agree with our new identity and purpose in Christ or we are fighting against our union with the bridegroom. We are basking in the love and affection of our relentlessly loving and caring Father, or we are frantically seeking knowledge and obedience of rules.

It is only through relationship that union and covenant are entered. Jesus wants to be one with us through a process of the intimate 'knowing' of us through conversation and experience. He adores living life with us. He IS love and created us with free will for the sake of love.

We are His beloved and our relationship, our union with the Trinity, where he who is joined to the Lord is one spirit with Him (1 Corinthians 6:17), is the priority over all else. Everything our Father does is relational. He came to be one with us, to make His home with us. He sent Jesus as the bridegroom with the church as His beautiful bride. He declares us as His children, heirs; He has made clear He is our Father made in His image. The intimacy He declares throughout His word yearns for relationship with us.

"And this is eternal life that they know you the only true God and Jesus Christ whom you have sent. I glorified you on earth, having accomplished the work that you gave me to do" (John 17:3-4).

We glorify the Father by our actions, by what we do. But eternal life, our abundant life, our freedom in the spiritual realm, comes through knowing God the Father, Jesus the Son, and the Holy Spirit of God in an intimate love relationship.

Our union with the Father, which joins us in perfect unity, comes through a love relationship initiated by the Father and embraced by His children.

33

KNOW WHEN

A man's wisdom gives him patience; it is to his glory to overlook an offense (Proverbs 19:11).

"But I say, walk by the Spirit, and you will not gratify the desires of the flesh ... if we live by the Spirit, let us also keep in step with the Spirit" (Galatians 5:16, 25).

In both parenting and every other relationship we encounter, there will be moments where children do not obey or other people don't meet our expectations. We have a choice in how to respond; we can respond with patience, allowing us to walk and live by the Spirit, or we can react in the flesh, usually involving anger.

Some situations are black and white, others require patience and wisdom. If we expect 100% obedience from our children every time we tell them to do something, as well as good responsible choices outside of direct guidance, we will live a life of frustration, anger, and disappointment as a parent.

For freedom Christ has set us free (Galatians 5:1). Freedom is not being able to do whatever we want. Freedom, in Christ, is making the right choice and abiding in Jesus. "Therefore, do not submit again to a yoke of slavery" (Galatians 5:16). The joy and life we find in the freedom is when we choose to walk by the Spirit, keeping in step with Him.

We take our children out of their freedom in Christ when we force them under our own law. Rather than a Spirit of sonship, we come at them with a spirit of you 'should know better than that and obey everything I say as well as what I think'! Ridiculous! Yes, but at some level it's true in our relationships with our children and other people.

"You are severed from Christ, you who would be justified by the law (or impose this on our children); you have fallen away from grace" (Galatians 5:4). We cannot lead our children into a love relationship with Jesus Christ when we justify them by our laws. That is, we respond to them based on their performance or obedience, because we pull them out of grace and nullify their freedom in Christ Jesus by making them slaves to our laws, our expectations of them.

We must learn, by abiding in Christ and walking in step with the Spirit, to 'Know When'. Know when we are majoring in the minors. Know when we are disciplining in pride because their current behavior reflects poorly on our roles as a parent; know when we are exasperating our children (Ephesians 6:4); know when they need grace, the empowering presence of God, in a situation. Know when love, a perfect love, is necessary to drive out the fear rather than harsh words; know when abounding love trumps identification of disobedience. We must know when their stepping into freedom is more important than stifling directions given in our fear as parents. We need to know when to empower our children with choice, teaching them how to live in the freedom they will have in Christ as adults.

Know when the mess or silly choice is not a big deal, but the anger waiting to address them is. Know when to overlook the little things, trusting in the Father to teach our children as well. Know when to stop the teaching, reprimanding, or disciplining and wrap the child in your arms and just hold them, because the loving-kindness of God leads us to repentance (Romans 2:4). Know when to pursue the heart of our children, peeling back the layers like an onion to see the wounds and where the Holy Spirit wants to bring healing.

We raise our children to live from a personal relationship with Jesus Christ through a disciplined life of obedience to the daily ministry of the Holy Spirit. We teach them to walk in step with the Spirit which leads to a life of freedom fed by grace. "For in Christ Jesus neither circumcision no uncircumcision (that is the law) counts for anything, but only faith working through love" (Galatians 5:6).

34

MY PLACE OF WORK

My work does not define me. Who I am is not dictated by the time I spend and the position I hold that pays my wages. My place of work is where God has presently placed me to influence others and make God known. My work is where and how my Father wishes to train me to reflect Jesus Christ in all that I do. My work does not give me my self-worth. My work does not place me in a social status or category. My work does not make me who I am and it does not determine how others see me.

These are simply lies set forth by the enemy to take my focus off of the eternal and off of Jesus. The enemy wants to determine how I see myself and how others see me. He can't do it! He does not have the power, influence, or authority to tell us who we are or what we are worth … unless we allow that … NEVER!

Our work is a place of influence for God's plans and purposes. Our Father has already accepted us and He doesn't operate as the world does. We are crucified to the world and the world is crucified to us (Gal 6:14) so they have no influence over us. God determines how people see us. He determines how people view us and what they think of us.

"Then the Lord said to Moses, 'See, I have made you like God to Pharaoh ... (Exodus7:1) and I will harden Pharaoh's heart (Exodus 7:3) ... but I raised you (Pharaoh) up for this very purpose, that I might show you my power and that my name might be proclaimed in all the earth'" (Exodus 9:16).

God has a plan and reason for our work, for where we are and what we do. It is about His goodness, kindness, and mercy, and to display His name. It is to make Him known. Our work is not about us. Our work is not about the temporary, the temporal, or the mist that is our life; being nothing more than a flash in an eternal timeline.

For us to place our worth or focus on our job is to completely miss it and waste an opportunity to give our lives an eternal purpose that could eternally change and affect the lives of countless people for the kingdom of heaven. How we make money is about how God wants to use us to bless His name and carry out the Great Commission.

35

NEVER DEFEATED

Defeat is in the heart and/or mind, not in the seen. Is death defeat? Is the loss of position or authority defeat? Who defines defeat?

What if these are points of transition the Lord uses to teach us, to take us into new positions, to give us new fresh authority, and carry us into abounding seasons of love and grace and testing and growth? What if our idea of defeat, failure, and loss, our perspective of these things, came from and were defined by the world instead of God?

What the enemy calls defeat the Lord uses for good. What the enemy calls beaten and defeated the Father calls humble and broken, ready for the next miracle and dose of power. God chose the weak and dumb of the world that others would call defeated. These are who He calls overcomers, champions, heirs, sons, and daughters.

We don't determine defeat for ourselves or others, no matter how evident it may appear. False conclusions of a person or event birth false, negative perspectives that draw us out of the peace of God and can shut down His flow. Negativity and defeat destroy faith, trust, belief, and hope. The enemy came to steal, kill, and destroy. Jesus came to bring abundant life and destroy the works of the devil.

Defeat is served only by the Lord to the enemy. Jesus has overcome the world. Defeat is not a reality for us as children of God. Our God works all things for the good of those who love Him and are called according to His purpose.

When we screw up; when we, by the world's (our friends, spouses, family, etc.) standards, 'fail' a task, school, test, etc., then we feel defeated. When we lose our temper, recognize self-pity, or show anger towards others, we are certain it's at least a temporary defeat in the eyes of the Lord.

If it were God's will for us to have a mindset of defeat then how could it also be His will for us to be joyful always, praying continually, and giving thanks in all circumstances? For this is God's will for us in Christ Jesus (1 Thessalonians 5:16-18).

God is not double minded about His love for us, His view toward us, or His intentions. He is unchanging in His love nature toward us. He poured out every ounce of wrath on Jesus so that the world could be reconciled to Him with redemption for those chosen to receive His free gift of salvation by grace through faith.

We are called in James to not be double-minded, that is, living in defeat rather than from victory, unstable in our thinking and actions.

We are eternally victorious in Christ Jesus, living, speaking, and moving from victory. We rise from glory to glory, born and bred to forcefully advance God's kingdom in the name of Jesus through the power of the cross.

We are in the first phase of our eternal life, which is but a mist, a vapor, and is a training ground for the future. Every facet of our being is made to walk in victory as we love God and love others. So let us believe in the hope set before us and take joy in our glorious Lord and Savior Jesus Christ!!

36

NO ONE IS GOOD

I asked the Father how it is that people without Him are still nice, great, happy people. Why am I such a mess and so depraved but others can be good?

Sin does not have to manifest itself in being bad, mean, selfish, lustful, etc. It does in you because that draws you away from the Lord and when given in, it creates shame and guilt. These are powerful weapons the enemy uses to bind up believers.

For some who don't know the Lord, the best deterrent Satan uses to keep them from God is to leave them alone so they think they are happy, content, and 'good' apart from Him. No one is good (Luke 18:19, Romans 3:10), but Jesus has reconciled the world to Himself. So there is no anger or judgment towards them. Jesus not only took the place of that, but He comes to their and your defense as an advocate for you (1 John 1:1-2). No matter how happy and content people appear there is no peace apart from Christ. People are tormented by their own demons. People do not understand or believe because of lies about God and also concerning who they are in this world.

You can tell Jesus' disciples by their fruit. We don't look for the absence of bad but the presence of good. It is not about the absence of sin but the presence of God. When the Father begins calling people to Him, their hearts and minds are opened and they begin to understand their depravity apart from Him. Not fully, by any means, but the knowledge of their own inability to be satisfied.

Good is a condition of the heart and mind that is open to the Father's heart. Good is His presence rising up on the inside and brilliantly eradicating the darkness. His presence emits an abundance of light and wind that shines into every dark corner and blows through the caverns of their souls.

We don't know what we don't know. People think they are good and happy and content the way they are. Just as a baby born in a prison never knowing a different life thinks he is free. People don't even know there is more because they are unaware of their own ignorance. But then someone hears about people who are "free", out of the prison they've always known, and they become aware that there may be more. People hear that the "free" people are worse off, at least some of them; that they do not have food or clothes and that the life they are living is no better, even worse than their life in prison.

The conclusion is drawn that their present situation is good, safe, certain, and they understand it. It is not risky and it requires no work, understanding, or further discovery on their part. They go through life believing they are living the life they were intended to live.

37

PASSION

Our passion is only limited by, and a reflection of, our love for God. Passion is birthed from love and produces a boldness while demolishing a fear of man. Passion sets us apart from those around us. Passion leads us to step out in faith. Passion is such a deep love and yearning for God that we gladly, joyfully abandon all else.

As perfect love drives out all fear (1 John 4:18), so passion birthed from love leads us to cry out to our Lord uncontrollably; to have to worship Christ as a release of the pressure built up within. Inside of passion our worship is spontaneous, pure acts of joy as we try to express our gratitude and thanks and love to our Savior for His love, joy, life, mercy, grace, forgiveness, and passion that is found in Him and Him alone.

38

PERCEPTION VS. REALITY

We constantly see through a certain lens and have "fallback" thoughts in response to comments, people, and circumstances. How we see a circumstance, others or ourselves is a perception, not a reality. But we often think that the thoughts running through our heads are the truth which is not always the case.

Our thoughts are influenced to say the least. They are created, molded, and impacted by what we have been taught, what we have experienced, and the specific world around our own life. We are influenced by the words and actions of others, our beliefs, Satan's influence, and most importantly the Holy Spirit's voice as the Father draws us to Jesus.

We are constantly sifting through these thoughts to determine how we will respond to circumstances, and to the thoughts of others as well. The way we think has a profound impact on every moment of our day. How we choose to interpret thoughts and situations will dictate how we think, what we see, and therefore our responses moment by moment.

Case in point: my wife says, "You could come sit by me on the couch and hold my hand. You haven't done that since you returned from your trip and I've asked you to a lot." This one statement can be interpreted and responded to in many different ways. The timing of when it's said, the tone (how she says it), the chosen words, the relevance of it, the truthfulness of each part of the statement, the perception of her motives, previous interactions between us that day, past comments, my personal mood and feelings towards her at that moment, Satan's lies and influence, if my crucified flesh flares up, and what the Spirit is saying are some of the factors that mold and impact my thoughts on the situation. These lead to a response based on my perception of my wife's comment and how I perceive the statement, how I perceive her, the situation, and myself.

My perception, right or wrong, becomes both my and my wife's reality once I respond or react. That doesn't make it true in that situation, but it does create another set of perceived thoughts up for analysis by another slew of lenses by which it will inevitably be viewed. We are constantly, and a lot of times unconsciously, viewing the world through the lens of our personal upbringing and experiences. We make judgments, categorize people, assess where we stand in a relationship, and determine our advantage and what we have to gain from people. We stop listening in conversations as we wonder what they think of us and what we're going to say in response to them. Past experiences have already begun to shape our view of people we meet and the situations we encounter.

We live by our perceptions, which are our views based on conclusions we have drawn, which determine our thoughts and the way we think. We have a choice of how we see and respond to every person and situation we find ourselves with. We have a choice. We have the power to choose how we look at every person and situation, thereby determining the thought process that will follow. We choose …

Apart from Christ, our ability to choose wisely is greatly diminished and will seldom if ever be the truth of a situation or about a person. We can choose to look through our tainted lens or through the lens of Jesus, seeing the Truth of a situation and person.

So "do not be conformed to this world, but be transformed by the renewal of your mind, that by testing you may discern what is the will of God, what is good and acceptable and perfect" (Romans 12:2).

We can be transformed through the way we think. Let's make clear we are not speaking to positive thinking apart from Christ. What we are exploring is the Truth that the Holy Spirit breathing into our hearts will explode in us; empowering us to walk in the freedom and life we are created for in Christ Jesus. This allows us to see in the spirit and process with the mind of Christ. This allows us to view ourselves, others and our circumstances in a whole new light that will forever change the way we think.

But we have the mind of Christ (1 Corinthians 2:16)! The Spirit searches everything, even the depths of God (1 Corinthians 2:10b). For who knows a person's thoughts except the spirit of that person, which is in him? So also no one comprehends the thoughts of God except the Spirit of God. Now we have received not the spirit of the world but the Spirit who is from God, that we might understand the things freely given us by God (1 Corinthians 2:12).

We have immense power in the freedom of choice our Savior has given us. Through the Spirit, we learn to think like Jesus, talk like Jesus, pray like Jesus, even fight like Jesus! The Spirit in us, the same one who raised Jesus from the dead, leads us into all Truth! He glorifies Jesus through us. He reminds us of the words of Jesus. He compels us through undeniable love. He empowers us to think from a mind of life and peace (Romans 8:6) and to be witnesses to the living Christ in our homes, work, cities, states, countries, and to the ends of the earth.

The Spirit opens the eyes of our hearts to know what is the hope to which He has called us (Ephesians 1:18). A mind set on the Spirit is life and peace. We may rejoice in hope, be patient in tribulation, and constant in prayer (Romans 12:12).

39

PERSPECTIVE: OVERLOOKING AN OFFENSE

When I become stressed, anxious, worried, frustrated, angry, impatient, prideful, or insecure, these relate to my identity. They are not who I really am. They are either my flesh, the old man who has already been put to death by Christ, or they are warfare from the enemy. Either way, they stem from a false perception I have of myself in Christ. We are transformed by the renewing of our minds (Romans 12:2).

So then, when my bride is short, disrespectful, angry, selfish, prideful, stressed, or tired, then it is not really her acting this way. In this case, it is her old self, warfare by the enemy, or ... my perception of her words or actions.

My first act of spiritual worship is to quickly ask to see and hear her as Jesus sees and hears her. So I must take the role of a servant before her. This does not conform to the pattern of the world, but it transforms me before her eyes through the renewing of my mind.

My next spiritual act of worship, and simultaneously slaughtering the enemy, is to speak life into who she really is in

Christ. This is an opportunity to fight for my wife. She is under opposition. I can put her deeper into it by reacting defensively in anger or ... I can fight for my bride and avenge her, send the old man back to the grave and send the enemy running in fear.

Here is a lens change, a different perspective that transforms us through the renewing of our mind. Responding in love and humility, overlooking an offense, is not allowing that person to win or be right, it is battling hell and valiantly fighting what is behind that person, and that which is lying to them.

When we act in accordance with the world then someone is lying to us about who we are in Jesus Christ or who God is for us. We must learn to protect those we love; fight for those we love by speaking into who they are in Christ, by taking such a place of humility that we can't be offended or put down. We rely on and know the Holy Spirit as our Comforter that we might have no insecurities in what others say or do (1 Corinthians 4:3-4).

Overlooking an offense is a victory over the enemy.

OVERLOOKING AN OFFENSE IS A VICTORY OVER THE ENEMY!

So I must choose - will I fight my beloved or will I fight the enemy? Will I fight FOR my beloved or will I fight FOR the enemy?

40

PERSPECTIVE: LENS CHANGE

We must understand that just because we have been taught or always believed something to be true, that it really is the truth or even right. The majority of people around us believing something does not make it true, it makes it popular. People voting something into law does not make it right or true, it simply means it won the vote. But how many of us know that just because something is popular does not make it right or true?

In the movie Shutter Island, they go through a whole role-playing masquerade in an attempt to reveal the truth to a patient at a psych ward. At the end of it he realizes the truth, he states reality, and at that moment he receives a new perspective that is the truth. He is freed from the delusions and lies he had been living in that were tormenting him, making him a prisoner not only in thought but also in the real world.

He receives a new perspective, he sees the truth, and he is living in freedom. The next morning, the doctor sits down beside him and asks him one question. By the answer given it is clear the patient forsook the freedom he had been given with his new and true perspective for his old one that was more comfortable.

He knew his old perspective. It was so embedded in him that he believed it was the truth and was unwilling to let it go because of the massive adjustment and work to keep the new perspective.

Sometimes a new lens can be painful, uncomfortable, and even difficult to comprehend because it may contradict what we have always known. It may reveal something that requires a huge shift in our lives. It may lead us to sever relationships, quit jobs, start new or different careers, step out in faith, and get out of our comfort zone. A new lens is required for growth. The way we look at Jesus impacts everything we do. The way we see ourselves, the Bible, and others will either hinder our pursuit of Christ or propel us into His will.

You can never change what you are not willing to confront.

If we are not willing to let go of beliefs, perspectives, and views we have always known to be true, then we cannot receive the new perspective God wants to give us.

So it is with us. God will give us a new lens to view Him, others, ourselves, or a situation. Then through revelation and experience we see through it, we get a taste of truth in that moment. But then we are not willing to let go of the conflicting perspective that has been true, not the truth, but true in our lives, for so long.

We have to let go and stop looking through one lens for us to receive and look through the new lens that Jesus wants to give us.

When our experience with God supersedes our historical view then we have to get a lens change in order to carry on the work that God has begun in our lives.

Desperation births belief.

When the Holy Spirit gives us a new perspective our hearts must change to go there, our minds must change to stay there, and our language must change for us to share from that place.

This is why Paul prays in Ephesians for the church to have the eyes of their hearts enlightened, to know the hope to which they have been called; to know the riches of the glorious inheritance he has set aside for them. For the eyes of their hearts to be opened, that is their spiritual lens, their perspective must align with Christ, they may know the immeasurable greatness of His power toward those who believe, according to the working of His great might (Ephesians 1:18-19).

41

POSSIBILITIES

We just believe that with God all things are possible: the abundant life He came to give, peace that transcends all understanding and guards our hearts and minds, the kingdom that is <u>not a matter of talk but of power,</u> a perfect love that drives out all fear, the mind of Christ, the same Holy Spirit in us that raised Jesus from the dead.

Jesus did great things on earth and said that we would do greater things than these: learning about God through experience, having a personal love relationship with our heavenly Father, hearing and knowing the voice of the Lord, loving our wives as Christ loves the church, raising our children to be fully devoted followers of Christ who love Jesus with all their heart, healing the sick and depressed, bringing new life to those who are dead or stale, speaking spirit and truth in love and grace that actually changes the heart of those who receive it and redirects their life.

We believe we are no longer struggling with sin, as Jesus dealt with sin once for all, but getting on the offensive and taking the fight against the enemy and storming the gates of hell! We live and walk in <u>authority</u> and power through the Spirit given us that is not of fear, but love, power, and self-control. We live in freedom, being joyful always, and giving thanks in all circumstances.

This is just a taste of what Jesus wants to do in and through us on earth as it is in heaven!!

What if there is more?

Are you and I living the abundant life Jesus came to give us?

Do we live in a peace that guards our hearts and minds in Christ Jesus?

Do we rejoice always, pray continually, and give thanks in all circumstances ... for this is God's will for you in Christ Jesus?

Acts 1:8 "But you will receive power when the Holy Spirit has come upon you, and you will be my witnesses in Jerusalem and in all Judea and Samaria, and to the end of the earth."

42

POWER AND MAJESTY
IN RESISTANCE

My power and majesty are seen in the resistance you experience in life. My beauty is all around you, and I am IN all the beauty. All creation reflects My glory. With the right lens, all of My majesty shines forth all around you. See Me and you will unlock the unlimited.

He draws us to the wilderness, to isolation with Him for a restoration of relationship, primarily in trust and confidence. He builds us up in the wilderness so we live from a place of trust in Him and confidence in who He is for us, in the city, town, etc. We must constantly be retreating to the wilderness for trust and confidence. A fresh filling up in Him. This is vital and revitalizing.

The River flows, the water churns
Blazing its own path
The water does not conform
The current flows
Rocks and resistance give way
The River runs

The earth beneath the water creates caps and waves
>   But the strength of the River presses on
Spirit of God
>   Flowing like the River
Living Water
>   Flow through me
Majestic King
>   Let your current go
Living Water
>   Mold me to you
Strong and magnificent
>   Your beauty is seen
The revelation of your love
>   All around me
You gave us this beauty
>   To magnify you
Open us up
>   To receive your love

43

SACRIFICIAL LOVE

Jesus sacrificed Himself for the world, but God's chosen people, the Israelites, rejected the Cornerstone. Jesus was rejected and killed by those who should have loved Him the most. Their perspectives were wrong. The way they thought about and perceived Jesus and the circumstances surrounding Him were inaccurate. These inaccurate views determined how they thought.

Rather than being transformed by the renewing of their minds they held onto their traditions, suppositions, and false beliefs. It was easy and safe to remain in the mindset of what they had always known, unwilling to see the Truth and accept the mind of Christ.

Jesus did not allow the hatred, unbelief, and rejection by His chosen people to deter Him from loving and giving Himself up for her. Their constant slander and mistreatment of Him had no effect on His cleansing and washing of her in order to present her to Himself in splendor, without spot or blemish.

He did not see His people as they were, but through the lens of unconditional love so that He could bring her into holiness, without blemish. Jesus was persecuted by His bride, beaten by His bride, rejected, and slandered, misunderstood, and ultimately killed on a cross by His bride. He kept His focus on His Father, through the Holy Spirit, so that He could look past the temporal and see the eternal. He loved His bride because His Father deserved to have His love, not because His bride earned or deserved His love.

Jesus was so full of the Holy Spirit and overflowing with love that He could actually love those who rejected Him. His focus was not on Himself but on the Father, in relationship with the Holy Spirit. In spite of ridicule and rejection, Jesus nourished and cherished His bride that He may present her in splendor before the Father, without spot or wrinkle, holy and without blemish.

Jesus came to serve, not to be served. Jesus came to fight for the very people He knew would reject Him. Jesus came to destroy the works of the devil, that is, the one who is behind the lies and destruction that influence the world and His bride. Jesus lives eternally with unconditional love for His people. In fact, God IS love. God did not just give us a thing called love, He gave us His Son who IS love and the Way, the Truth, and the Life; then filled us with His Spirit of love, power, and self-control.

Where sin is present grace abounds all the more. The empowering presence of God that enables us to become the people God already sees when He looks at us. We were created to love by our Father who IS love, that we may love others; especially our enemies, those who reject us, not just with word or talk but in deed and truth. For when we love one another God abides in us and His love is perfected in us (1John 4:12). His perfect love drives out our fleshly fear, that through our love for the Father we love our brother.

Jesus defeated the enemy through sacrificial love. He let go of every part of Himself so that He, fully surrendered to the Father and the ministry of the Holy Spirit, might display the Father's love for us. He overcame evil with good. He took the slander, the beatings, the mocking, the torture, and death so that He could envelop every sin committed and forgiving all the while, make way for us to come to the Father.

We, through a love that denies self, open the door to display the love of Christ, glorifying the Father, and overcoming evil with good.

But if when you do good and suffer for it you endure, this is a gracious thing in the sight of God. For to this, you have been called, because Christ also suffered for you, leaving you an example, so that you might follow in His steps. He committed no sin, neither was deceit found in His mouth. When He was reviled (spoken to abusively), He did not revile in return; when He suffered, He did not threaten but continued entrusting Himself to Him who judges justly. He himself bore our sins in His body on the tree, that we might die to sin and live to righteousness (1 Peter 2:20b-24).

"Fear not, stand firm and see the salvation of the Lord ... the Lord will fight for you, and you have only to be still (silent)" (Exodus 14:13-14).

"A man's wisdom gives him patience, it's to His glory to overlook an offense" (Proverbs 19:11).

44

SALT OF THE EARTH

In order to be the salt of the earth (Matt 5:13) and the light of the world (Matthew 5:14), we must keep our eyes fixed on the eternal; focused on Jesus, the author, and perfecter of our faith (Hebrews 12:2). We cannot be lukewarm. We cannot serve two masters (Matthew 6:24). A divided kingdom cannot stand.

We seek first the kingdom of heaven and His righteousness (Matthew 6:33). We let go of our desires and perspectives of every situation. Rather, we actively crucify and put to death our own will and perspective so that we might train in godliness to focus on the eternal. We seek the Father's will and Jesus' perspective in every circumstance.

As we beat our bodies and make them our slaves, we are alive in Christ through His glorious grace and majesty. It is in this place of self-surrender and submission that Christ in us rises from the depth of our souls and His spirit ignites a flame that effects true, eternal change in our lives.

We come to know the Spirit through experience and we fan the flame into a raging fire. It ignites everything in us to pursue

God's plans and purposes in our lives with a fresh vigilance that sets us apart from the world around us and shines the light of Jesus in the darkened places He sets in our paths.

So send the Fire Lord!

45

SIGNS UNDENIABLE (FAITH)

"For that a notable sign has been performed through them is evident to all the inhabitants of _____, and we cannot deny it" (Acts 4:16).

Our Father performs signs, wonders, and miracles to show that He is our God. The one true God, high and lifted up. His ways are not our ways, but higher, and His thoughts are not our thoughts, but higher (Isaiah 55:8). The people will know that He is God by the works of His hands.

Jesus made it clear the need and purpose for God's tangible power. "The works I do in My Father's name bear witness about me," (John 10:25) for "even though you do not believe me, believe the works, that you may know and understand that the Father is in me and I am in the Father" (John 10:38).

There are no barriers that the Cornerstone cannot crush and destroy. Jesus came to destroy the works of the devil (1 John 3:8); the enemy was conquered, and continues to be beaten and bruised, by the blood of the Lamb and word of our testimonies (Revelation 12:11), by the word of the testimony of those who see our Father perform works that cannot be denied. Works that cannot be explained by science or any other explanation outside of the Almighty's glorious hands.

So we must believe. We must encourage one another in our faith and cry out for an impartation of faith that was credited as righteousness. Faith is an enzyme, a catalyst that can catapult a movement in the heart of God to a pouring out of His glory to tangible works in our midst.

But woe to us and those who have no faith. In Jesus' hometown, He could not do mighty works, except the laying of hands on a few sick people, because of their unbelief (Mark 6:5-6). The disciples, after failing to heal a demon-possessed man, came to Jesus and asked why they couldn't do it, why they weren't seeing His hand. Jesus replied, "Because of your little faith … if you have faith the size of a mustard seed you will say to the mountain move from here to there and it will move, and nothing will be impossible for you" (Matthew 17:19-21).

"Now Jesus did many other signs in the presence of the disciples, which are not written in this book; but these are written so that you may believe that Jesus is the Christ, the Son of God and that by believing you may have life in His name" (John 20:30-31).

46

SOFTEN THE HEART

When we speak to someone, when it's from the heart with love, compassion, and grace, then it softens the heart of those we're speaking to. We naturally put up walls and become defensive when someone we feel doesn't have the right, position, authority, or experience to tell us something. Our defenses go up, hearts harden, and our minds start turning because our pride rises up.

But when we speak in obedience, out of love, never to be right or prove a point, then what comes out is not about us, but about God's love and wisdom. The loving, compassionate heart speaking the words of Christ in grace and love and humility softens the heart of others. It draws down defenses and puts them at ease that it is safe, that they are safe, there is nothing to prove, and it doesn't change the roles or relationship.

It's a gracious, loving word not about the person speaking it, but it is for God's glory to bring a taste of heaven to earth at that moment.

"The one who speaks on his own authority seeks his own glory, but the one who seeks the glory of Him who sent him is true, and in him, there is no falsehood" (John 7:18).

47

SOW INTO IT …

"The point is this: whoever sows sparingly will also reap sparingly, but whoever sows bountifully will also reap bountifully" (2 Corinthians 9:6).

We sow into the disciplines of our relationship with Christ. We pour into the people, places, and activities where we see our Father working. We follow Jesus with zeal and determination and violence of action. We reap what we sow: "Do not be deceived: God is not mocked, for whatever one sows, that he will also reap … so let us not grow weary of doing good, for in due season we will reap, if we do not give up" (Galatians 6:7-9).

If we want to see the Father work miraculously through us then we must sow into it. When we choose to live and walk in the flesh, He's not disappointed IN us, He's disappointed FOR us because He knows the plans He has for us, to prosper, to do good, to advance the kingdom of heaven.

It's not about what we must do, it's all about the heavenly response to and results of a heart and mind dedicated to Christ and sowing into a personal relationship with Jesus. It is about joining with all that heaven is doing.

We create an atmosphere that is irresistible to the Holy Spirit and all the upgrades that He and Jesus want to pour over us and raise up inside of us. We bring Christ into the room and He can't help but move in love and grace and goodness. That's His nature! He's madly sensitive to humility, surrender, and obedience. He's overcome with compassion when we sow into who He is for us as a result of what He's done for us. We reap what we sow because our Father has an irresistible desire to show us every day how much He loves and adores us. How much He loves to give us good gifts and pour out blessings and favor over us, His beloved children.

Ask and it will be given. Fathers give to sons, how much more will our heavenly Father give to those who ask (Matthew 7:7-11).

I think about my children. When I see them obey, it raises up love and compassion inside of me that is sub-conscious. I see them moving in grace and love and kindness and respect and it makes me want to pour out love and affection and gifts and adoration all over them. I will praise them, let them know how proud I am of them. Show them my appreciation for them with gifts, words, hugs, and kisses. It is not a formulated response like a reward. It's not watching a mouse go through a maze and giving a piece of cheese, or having a dog fetch a ball and giving it a treat. Those are conditional rewards based on directed behavior. What I am speaking of is the ever-present, unconditional love exploding in joy and love and adoration when love and respect are seen. It's not a choice response, it is an uncontrollable condition of the heart. That is what Jesus has towards us. It's not as though the Father thinks, "he obeyed my fifth command so now he will receive this gift or favor" - NEVER!

It's about a proud Father who loves His children so much and He overflows when He watches them do the right thing, make the right choice, respond in love, display humility, surrender a sin to Him and turnabout in repentance. His nature is holy; a righteousness that is so beyond overjoyed with His children when He watches them. He just really loves us. I can't adequately describe it in words, but I know it in my heart because it's how I feel towards my children. And then as I think about it, I know that what I feel for my children pales in comparison to the love He has for them and all His children and I just have to smile because life just became really good!

48

SPIRITUAL SURVIVAL

J
ust as there are necessities for surviving in the physical world, so too there are necessities for surviving in the spiritual realm.

The cross of King Jesus, dripping with His blood that covers us, takes away our sins and the separation from our heavenly Father.

The Holy Spirit. There is no survival without the gift of the Holy Spirit. Faith is the foundation of these things.

Love. Love is the root of creation. Love is what drives our Father and love is what must flow from us.

Hope. Hope is knowing that we serve a great and glorious God who is our Healer, Provider, Counselor, Teacher, etc.; whose unfailing love is unfathomable in our minds; whose love for us is never changing, never fading, and sacrificial at its core. Hope is knowing that our one true God will never leave us nor forsake us and nothing can ever separate us from His presence (Hebrews 13:5, Romans 8:39).

PMA (Positive Mental Attitude). Hope is our spiritual positive mental attitude, keeping our eyes fixed on Jesus, the eternal, and the things above.

Fire (Spark). The Holy Spirit is our fire. He brings us to life, instills hope, brings gifts and warmth, and teaches us.

Water. Jesus Christ is our water, without Him we are dead, we cannot survive. There is no other way, no other alternative. It is only accepting what Jesus Christ did that brings life that saves us.

Shelter. Faith is our shelter; it guards us against the attacks of both the world and the enemy. Without faith in God's words and promises we will succumb to the "elements".

Signal. Love is our signal. Love is how Jesus went to the cross. Love is how we see, know, and accept our Lord. Love is how we signal that we know God and is what is seen by those around us signaling we are not citizens of this world (Phil 3:20), but are surviving, even thriving, here until we reach our heavenly home.

Map/Guide. The Scriptures (2 Timothy 3:16-17).

Sleep. Rest and Peace in Christ Alone. It is critical.

We are surviving here on earth, but we have a mission to stay alive and keep others 'alive' until the King returns.

49

STARTING POINT FOR SPOUSE AND KIDS

Today, some of our greatest challenges are time and focus. We, along with our family, our children, are extremely busy and bombarded by an ever-increasing list of important tasks we must accomplish, activities we should do, truths we should learn, or teach others. Our focus becomes so divided it no longer produces results. Our lives quickly become complex, degrading our ability to do a few important things well.

This truth is evident within the nuclear family. Satan thrives in attacking our families, God's core of society. Family is the Lord's representation of Christ's relationship with the church and the primary place for the discipleship of our children. It is easy to lose our focus on what is vital in the lives of our spouses and children. There are so many distractions that muddy the waters with the hopes we will major on the minors and miss the heart.

Here is a starting point for us to return to in the fulfillment of Jesus' command to love God and love others. "Husbands, love your wives, as Christ loved the church and gave himself up for her, that He might sanctify her, having cleansed her by the washing of water with the word, so that He might present the church to Himself in splendor, without spot or wrinkle or any such thing, that she might be holy and without blemish." (Ephesians 5:25-27).

As men we are called to prepare our brides for the bridegroom by washing her in the word of God, sacrificing ourselves for her, and daily presenting her to our Lord in splendor (brilliant or gorgeous appearance of their heart as God does not look at the outward appearance, but at the heart (1 Samuel 16:7). See, our focus is to live out the kindness of God that leads her to repentance (Romans 2:4), overcoming evil with good (Romans 12:21), leading her into the righteousness she is given through Jesus.

This is a starting point for the focus of our children, especially as we see them beginning to live in their freedom, at risk of the world's influence in their lives. Outside influence by the world is inevitable. Our children must learn how to live in the freedom they have as sons/daughters of the Lord. Our children are first and foremost God's children, given to us as a blessing (Psalms 127:3-5), with the responsibility to flood them with the love of Christ leading them into a personal love relationship with Jesus. We must raise them up to know their true identity as children of the Most High God, heirs to the throne, warriors, and overcomers, more than conquerors! They were born for such a time as this, to walk with God in the glorious freedom He has given them, with wisdom in the midst of the tremendous power of choice.

Our focus on our children has been tainted. Clothes, sports, grades, hobbies, activities, instruments, special skills, and fulfilling their entitlement mentality have become idols. They have become our focus as parents. This list is by no means all-inclusive so as the Holy Spirit highlights other priorities in your children's lives acknowledge them so they can be returned to their rightful place. Our focus over all else with our children is to prepare them as the brides of Christ. They are God's children, and we are to present them in splendor (brilliant or gorgeous appearance of their heart as God does not look at the outward appearance but at the heart (1 Samuel 16:7). We do not focus on behavior modification (which never justifies a lack of discipline) but our target is the heart.

Paul tells us the Father pours His love into our hearts through the Holy Spirit (Romans 5:5). What if our priority as parents is to lead our children to a place to receive the Father's love through the Holy Spirit? What would it look like for us to intentionally put aside the distractions of our day to day lives and allow Jesus' kindness to lead our children to repentance through our words, thoughts, and actions? How much time do we devote to displaying the love of Jesus to our kids? Let us overcome evil with good.

It requires intentionality of cutting out the fat in our schedules, and the schedules of our children, to allow time, and the energy, to focus on what is important.

Let go of all the extracurricular activities; mandate dinners as a family to break bread and fellowship; and take priority over the excessive time spent with friends.

Touch the heart of your children. Speak life into them whenever you can.

Pray for the Holy Spirit to speak to you how He sees your children and what He loves and adores about them. Share that with them.

Speak into what is great about them rather than cutting them down for petty mistakes and character flaws.

Remember it is the kindness of God that leads us to repentance. Focus on the righteousness of your kids. If you want to see patience, rather than uncontrolled emotional responses in your children, then display patience, calmness, and peace to them.

Establish guard rails in who they spend time with, what they are watching, what electronic activities they are participating in. Win their hearts as a loving father and mother just as our heavenly Father has won our hearts.

Get extra sleep and time in the morning with the Father so you can better interact with your children and spouse. Let no unwholesome words come out of your mouth, but only that which is good for building up, as fits the occasion, that it may give grace to those who hear (Ephesians 4:29).

Wow, our words can give grace to those who hear them. That is, the empowering presence of God that enables us to become the people God already sees when He looks at us.

God sees present-future. If you talk with Him He is honored and ecstatic to share with you how He sees you, your spouse, your children, and others. He'll speak tenderly to what makes Him so proud and what He cannot wait to see further developed in our lives and the lives of our children. He loves to speak in spirit and truth to change the dynamic in our hearts and give us new perspectives of Him, ourselves, and others.

Our focus for our children must be to prepare them for their relationship with Jesus Christ. Depending on their age and what that currently looks like in their lives, this may require drastic changes or a continuation of your/their current paths. We must be intentional to cut away whatever does not lead them further into the heart of God and introduce a constant loving-kindness that teaches them who they are in Christ and how to live in the freedom they have in Him. So, our starting point ... tell your kids every day who they are in Christ, how He sees them, and allow the kindness of God to lead them into repentance.

50

STEWARDSHIP

"Everyone to whom much was given, of him, much will be required, and from him to whom they are entrusted much, they will demand the more" (Luke 12:48).

"Pay attention to what you hear: with the measure you use, it will be measured to you, and still more will be added to you. For the one who has, more will be given, and from the one who has not, even what he has will be taken away" (Mark 4:24-25).

"For to the one who has, more will be given, and he will have an abundance" (Matthew 13:12).

During the game of football, if a receiver keeps dropping the ball, the quarterback will stop throwing it to him. In the same way, if we are not stewards of what God gives us, He'll stop giving to us. He will not give us more because we have not proven that we are responsible with what He has given us. This has no relation to his love or goodness towards all of his children.

But if a receiver catches all the passes the quarterback throws, then the quarterback will throw to him more often and in more critical plays knowing that it will be a successful pass. This receiver will be used for the big wins, the great victories because he has proven himself trustworthy in all the other passes thrown his way. The best receivers will get the most opportunities and passes.

An abandoned life in Christ is not passively received, it is aggressively taken (Secrets of the Secret Place, p. 71).

51

STORMS

We don't respond correctly to storms, trials, and circumstances. We run FROM God to addictions, to getaways, anything to give us a reprieve, if but for a moment. Yet in Psalm 57 we cry out to God, for His mercy, and take refuge in the shadow of His wings, Him alone.

This requires an internal and external admission that He knows better, that we can't deal with it, but more importantly that we trust Him to deal with it. 'Deal with it' does not mean that He quells the storm, so we can't think of it that way; but that He touches us with peace, speaks a word of comfort, restores our faith, refreshes hope through a glimpse of His face or His hand.

We cannot think that we know best. We know nothing. Jesus spoke and did what the Father spoke and did. We could not possibly do anything different. It is humility, knowing our place before the Father, the Son, and the Holy Spirit, which allows us to be comforted and guided in the stale and lifeless moments of our lives. It is a recognition, through humility, of Christ in everyone and everything around us. In humility, how could I speak negatively about my heavenly Father's son or daughter: I don't know their past or future, but HE knows?

In humility, I must trust Him, in His love, and always in His everlasting, never-failing goodness. He works all things for the good of those who love Him and have been called according to His purpose (Romans 8:28). How arrogant of me to get mad at circumstances; to think it should be done, or would be better, this way instead of that way.

I realize, looking back on various seasons, how little I know and how small I am. Only in humility will we stop questioning God's plans and methods and trust in His love and goodness. Peace and comfort flow freely in trusting relationships.

52

TAKE THESE SINS

John of the Cross describes the dark night that is necessary for God to passively purify our hearts through uprooting sins. These may be sins that have long gone unnoticed until the time when the Spirit decides to take action against them (Devotional Classics, p.33).

When a weed or plant has deep roots, its removal is no small feat with no small impact on the ground it has penetrated. Sins that have taken deep roots in our heart are not easily removed. The ground must be softened with water; the heart must be softened with the Living Water, the Spirit.

The softening and extraction are a joint process within the dark night, for those sins that have deeply rooted themselves. Our bowing down in submission and surrender, rendering to the Spirit our helplessness, opens us to receive the love poured into our hearts through the Spirit (Romans 5:5).

We must be brought to our knees to receive the flood of Living Water necessary to initiate the removal of the deep-rooted sin. As the Spirit softens and extracts in the dark night He also prepares the replacement soil. A large root takes up a large space; when removed it leaves a hole, a void in our hearts. This must be filled in, lest the demon returns with his friends. The darkness is the purifying of the heart, but for the purpose of the presence of God more so than the absence of sin.

The removal of sin alone is not enough, the root is pulled for the purpose of creating space, and increasing the communion between God and man for more of His presence. The hole from the root must be filled with the seeds of the fruit of the Spirit.

In its place, the Spirit will grow in love, joy, peace, patience, kindness, goodness, gentleness, faithfulness, and self-control. He brings forth humility, contentment, and strength. We can rejoice at the recognition of the dark night in our lives, indicating God's work of death and life in us. Removing these sins to make room for more of Him.

53

THANKFUL PSALM

Psalm 70:4 "But may all who seek you rejoice and be glad in YOU; may those who love your salvation, always say, 'Let God be exalted!'"

Our Father has granted us and continues to grant us so many awesome and wonderful gifts, but above all, one to remember every day, is the gift of salvation through His Son Jesus Christ. That is what we find joy and peace in each and every day.

After the 72 returned they were so excited! They experienced the love and power of Jesus firsthand as they cast out demons, healed the sick, living out by faith the authority Jesus had given them: to trample on snakes and scorpions and overcome the power of the enemy! After all this they are in awe of God's power and Jesus says (paraphrased of course), yes, all of this is great and awesome, but more so than all of the gifts I want you to rejoice that your names are written in the Book of Life (Luke 10:20). Love the salvation that I bring and always say, 'Let God be exalted!' (Psalm 70:4).

When life seems to offer nothing to be thankful for, when a day comes that offers no light, and when situations arise that make us think there is no hope and we have no reason to smile or be glad, then on that day, in that moment, fix your eyes on Jesus, on the Eternal.

Trust in His sovereignty and unfailing love and take your rightful place with Christ in the heavenly realms. (Ephesians 2:6) Rejoice in the eternal gift that has raised you up in Christ, completely independent of our actions, of what we do or say, for it is by grace through faith, not by our works! (Ephesians 2:8)

Our eternal dwelling in the presence of God our Father is untouchable and unchangeable. Therefore, be joyful always, pray continually, and give THANKS in ALL circumstances for this is God's will for you in Christ Jesus (1 Thessalonians 5:16-18).

To be thankful is to be joyful!

54

RELEASE

I t is the Spirit who gives life, the flesh is no help at all. The words I have spoken to. You are spirit and life (John 6:63).

We host the Spirit of Christ and Jesus himself. We carry the Creator of the universe because he has chosen to dwell within us. He is so excited to make their home in us. To live in loving, amazing intimacy with every one of his children.

Our role in advancing the kingdom of heaven is to release heaven all around us. We host his presence, remain aware of him, and speak words that are spirit and life.

Sometimes we think we need to convince people about Jesus, but the flesh is no help at all. We may be under the impression the pressure to advance the kingdom is on our shoulders. Paul didn't think that way. He was aware that, although he was very educated having years of study equivalent to modern-day Bachelors, Masters, and Doctorates in all things God, he had to release heaven.

"My speech and my message were not in plausible words of wisdom, but in demonstration of the Spirit and of power, so that your faith might not rest in the wisdom of men but in the power of God (1 Corinthians 2:4-5). He said it this way to the church at Thessalonica, "...our gospel came to you not only in word but also in power and in the Holy Spirit and with full conviction (proof)" (1 Thessalonians 1:5).

The greatest gift we could bring to a friend, the greatest influence we could display to the world around us, is to release over them the Spirit and life of the kingdom. God works in the lives of people in many ways we will never see or understand. We can release the goodness of God, his presence, even his amazing grace into the atmosphere and lives around us, casting out the prince of the power of the air and ushering in the manifest presence of God.

"Let no corrupting talk come out of your mouth, but only such as is good for the building up, as fits the occasion, that it may give grace to those who hear" (Ephesians 4:29). The Father has empowered us with the authority to release grace, the empowering presence of God that enables us to become the people He already sees when He looks at us, into the lives of others when we are aligned with the Spirit.

Jesus described our role in releasing spirit and life. "Whoever believes in me, as the Scripture has said, 'out of his heart will flow rivers of Living Water (the Holy Spirit)" (John 7:38). Subsequently, "out of the abundance of the heart the mouth speaks" (Luke 6:45) and from the heart flows the wellspring of life (Proverbs 4:23).

We do not live under pressure to perform or to convince people, or change people's hearts or minds or behaviors. That is the work of the Holy Spirit. We live in his presence and release the Spirit in all his glory and goodness to those around us and into the atmosphere.

In the release of the Lord, hearts and minds are forever changed, lives are transformed, and people are redeemed, resurrected to new life. We do not live to convince; we release to bring life. We live lives soaked in his presence, aware of him all around us.

Presence and healing were released through Paul's clothing (Acts 19:12). The sick were brought to the path where Peter walked. They anticipated a release of the Spirit upon Peter for healing (Acts 5:15).

Release is how Jesus advances the kingdom through us. We have nothing to offer, but he has everything to give.

55

TRUST IN YOU LORD

Give the Lord your dreams and desires. Let go of expectations and unfounded entitlements. When you hold onto these then your natural reaction is fear when things do not align with them. Fear not! I am with you. Fear Not! For I know the plans I have for you. Trust in the Lord with all your heart and lean not on your own understanding. But in all things acknowledge Me and I will make your paths straight (Proverbs 3:5-6).

Trust is the acceptance of God and his goodness and THEN the letting go of your worries, concerns, plans, dreams, sense of entitlement, and expectations. It's not trusting everything will be great. It's not trusting things will go as planned. It's not trusting there will be no pain or loss or grief or hardship. We trust in who God is. We trust in His unchanging nature that is absolutely loving and kind, with our eternal interest at heart. We trust in His goodness. We trust in His promises that He has made.

These promises are interpreted by the mind of Christ (1 Corinthians 2:16) and viewed through the eternal, all-knowing, all-loving eyes of Jesus; NOT the world's perspective or interpretation. We keep our eyes fixed on Jesus, the author, and perfecter of our faith (Hebrews 12:2). We focus on the eternal, never the temporal. We trust in His lovingkindness in all things, but our focus and desires remain on Him.

We commit our work to the Lord and our plans will be established (Proverbs 16:3). Everything has been made by the Lord for a purpose, even the wicked (Proverbs 16:4) ... The heart of man plans his way, but the Lord establishes his steps (Proverbs 16:9). We go before the Lord even before we plan so that we align our hearts, minds, and desires with His will. It is in our Secret Place in rest and stillness before Him that we learn to trust in the Lord with all of our heart, not leaning on our own understanding (Proverbs 3:5).

It is in our failure to trust our Father that we become weary and heavily burdened. We take upon our shoulders the pressure of every circumstance and decision, striving for a cerebral understanding and the perfect decision.

Come to Me (your Good Shepherd) all who labor and are heavy laden, and I will give you rest. Take My yoke (trusting in His will to be done) upon you, and learn from Me, for I am gentle and lowly in heart, and you will find rest for your souls. For my yoke is easy and my burden is light (Matthew 11:28-30).

Proverbs 3:5 "Trust in the Lord with all your heart and do not lean on your own understanding."

56

UNLOCK THE UNLIMITED

"But one thing I do: forgetting what lies behind and straining forward to what lies ahead, I press on toward the goal for the prize of the upward call of God in Christ Jesus ... let us hold true to what we have attained" (Philippians 3:14,16).

God has a plan and purpose for each of us. He has a magnificent dream for us, bigger than anything we could ask or think (Ephesians 3:20). He is unlimited and lives in a place of possibilities. He has no box to think outside of because there was never an initial boundary.

Jesus said all things are possible with my glorious Father, just believe! Just Believe! We are constantly being trained, tested, and upgraded! We move from glory to glory in grace upon grace. That is, without measure, when we consciously and actively respond to the majestic Spirit of Christ in us.

We are training for reigning, learning how to partner with Jesus in bringing heaven in all of its glory here on earth. Our focus is on emulating Jesus, who responds to us saying, My Beloved, your unlimited potential is unlocked in My Spirit! You witnessed my life, but greater works than these will you do by My energy and My Spirit working powerfully within you. (John 14:12) He is able to do and accomplish far more than you could ask or imagine (Ephesians 3:20).

His Spirit is wonderful and magnificent. He loves to defy logic and reason in his adoration and development of your heart. He is so excited to walk with you every single day. He rejoices at the prospect of the righteousness He gets to build up in you. His focus is on your heart beloved, the wellspring of life (Proverbs 4:23).

Give Him your heart each day, walk in the Spirit with Him. (Galatians 5:16) It is not easy nor is this path comfortable. But Jesus calls you to live as the citizen of heaven that you are (Philippians 3:20) which will never make sense here on earth. But one thing you must do as his children: strain forward to what lies ahead, press on toward the upward call. Unlock the unlimited in your life.

Everything else is put aside, even good things. You must throw off everything that hinders, and the sin that so easily entangles, and run with endurance the race set before you (Hebrews 12:1). The level you go to in your relationship with the Spirit of Christ is limitless. He has such plans for us, but you must respond and set everything else aside. Jesus is asking to be your everything. He says, Give Me your heart My beloved and you will see heaven all around you. Give Me your desires, your dreams, your wants, your family, and friends. Lay at My feet your job and hobbies and your religion. Let My Spirit teach you what is right, not religious traditions or men with their own agendas.

As fast and violently as you move forward in the kingdom so will you come to love the process and receive your inheritance, through your identity in Jesus, to unlock the unlimited? Restrictions and caps and constraints are earthly mindsets put forth by men out of fear and a desire to control what they do not understand. Jesus wants your mistakes to be in too much belief and too much faith; believing in him too much and praying huge prayers.

Don't dwell in fear and unbelief. I, the Alpha and Omega, powerfully dwell in you. My Spirit is in you. Join Me in violently advancing the kingdom and live in the reality of seeing heaven here on earth. Unlock the unlimited.

Ephesians 3:20 "Now to him who is able to do far more abundantly than all that we ask or think, according to the power at work within us."

57

WEEDS AND VIRUSES, THE HEALING PROCESS

You can cut the top off a weed and it seems to be gone. But a week later, maybe a month, maybe only a day or a few hours it's back. A root is living and resilient, giving cause for our perseverance. If we do not get to the roots then it's not really gone. Pulling off the leaves of the root is just the first battle; it will ALWAYS come back if we stop there. We must kill its roots. It may be a process depending on how deep the roots go, requiring multiple occasions of pulling and cutting it and constant attention.

So it is with sin in our lives. We genuinely repent of it, surrender it, and by God's power and grace, we are healed. However, the leaves of the root above the surface have just been pulled. Sin is resilient so we must have perseverance (Romans 5:3-4, James 1:2-4). That was the first battle.

The second battle is digging deep via the Holy Spirit to discover the root.

Ask questions for Him to reveal the root. Ask many questions and wait and pray and ask and pray and ask and wait and pray.

Ask for forgiveness for people in the past (anything that came up, even if it does not feel like it would have had any impact) and then we forgive ourselves.

Continue the process, bringing everything that comes to mind before God

> The third battle is life changing once that is discovered.
> Make deliberate choices and changes.
> Find one or more men/women for accountability, because we were not created to live life alone (James 5:16, Proverbs 27:17, Proverbs 28:13).
> Daily die to yourself and sin (Luke 9:23) to prevent the return in your flesh and to keep the enemy from establishing a foothold.
> Be constant in the worship of who God is for us, his unchanging nature, and what He has already done for us and promises to do.

Jesus has already won this victory for us.

Weeds, viruses, cancer, they all start very benign, tiny, nearly unnoticeable. When they are not caught early, or they are fed in small ways, they get out of control before we know it and there is so much damage done that it seems irreversible.

If we give our flesh, or the devil an inch they will take a mile ... But if we give GOD an inch (make time for Him every day, obey, worship) he'll take us a thousand miles!!

2 Corinthians 10:3-5 "For though we walk in the flesh, we are not waging war according to the flesh. For the weapons of our warfare are not of the flesh but have divine power to destroy strongholds. We destroy arguments and every lofty opinion raised against the knowledge of God, and take every thought captive to obey Christ."

58

WHO I AM

I am alive in Christ Jesus (1) living in the fullness of His love and grace. Grace is the empowering presence of God that enables me to become the man/woman God already sees when He looks at me. The fullness of God the Father, the Holy Spirit, and Jesus dwell in me (2) because I abide in Christ and him in me. I am dead to sin (3) and I have been crucified to the world (4). Neither of them has a hold on me nor influence over me. I am a new creation (5), born again, and the old, sinful self is dead.

Jesus Christ died as me, so also I was raised with Christ in newness of life (6). When I resurrected with Jesus Christ, I became pure, blameless, righteous, and free from accusation (7). I am a saint, I am no longer a sinner because, though I sin, I do not take ownership of it (8) and it does not define who I am.

I am a son/daughter of the Most High God, heir to the throne of the One True King, a servant to a lost world, alive in Christ, dead to sin. I will lay my life down daily for my Lord and Savior (9). Jesus became for me the wisdom of God - my righteousness, holiness, and redemption (10).

My Father has blessed me with every spiritual blessing and chosen me to be holy and blameless before I was born (11). I am loved, I am accepted, I am clean, I am worthy, and I am free!

1) Romans 6:11, Ephesians 2:5

2) Colossians 2:9–10

3) Romans 6:11

4) Galatians 6:14

5) 2 Corinthians 5:17

6) Romans 6:4, Colossians 2:12

7) Colossians 1:22, 1 Corinthians 1:30

8) Romans 7:17, 20

9) Luke 9:23

10) 1 Corinthians 1:30

11) Ephesians 1:3, 4

59

WHY HAVE JOY?

I have given you authority to trample on snakes and scorpions and to overcome ALL the power of the enemy; nothing will harm you. However, do not rejoice that the spirits submit to you, but rejoice that your names are written in heaven (Luke 10:19-20). We don't have to be the greatest husband or see people turn to God daily, or receive revelations, or heal the sick, or raise the dead to have a reason to rejoice and be joyful.

Our joy is not circumstantial. Nor is it an emotion based on how we feel. Everything can be going wrong and we still have a reason for joy ... our names are written in the Book of Life. Our names are written in heaven! We will spend eternity in the presence of God! Be anxious about nothing, but bring everything before God (Philippians 4:6). Cast all your anxiety on Him because He cares for you (1 Peter 5:7). Not just the big things, but all things, everything!!! Then allow the peace of God, which transcends all understanding, to guard your hearts and minds in Christ Jesus (Philippians 4:7).

I praise you because I am fearfully and wonderfully made (Psalm 139:14). I run in the path of your commands, for you have set my heart free (Psalm 119:32) and I lift up my hands for your commands, which I love (Psalm 119:48).

Our joy and peace are not a result of our thoughts or actions. We don't earn joy. We express joy because of what Christ has already done. If nothing else productive for the kingdom happened in our lives, we would still have a reason for joy. We have the living, loving, powerful Holy Spirit within us, so we have joy!

Joy cannot be attained by anything this world has to offer. There comes in our joy a love, which comes from God. It's because of what He has done, not us that makes the atmosphere around us more like Christ. We create room for Him. This astounds and mystifies those around us. This joy exposes them to the Holy Spirit and thwarts the efforts of the ruler of the air (Ephesians 2:2), that is the evil one who works in those who are disobedient. Do you see this beautiful dynamic of how our amazing God pours out his Grace on all? Rejoice in the Lord, be joyful, give thanks in all circumstances ... ALWAYS (1 Thessalonians 5:16-18, Philippians 4:4)!

60

WHO YOU ARE

W ho you are is not determined by what you do or don't do. I established you in my kingdom before you were born. I chose you. When I look at you I see nothing wrong with you. My goodness flows over and through you constantly. I determine how people see you and view you. Who you are is based on who I am for you and through you. Humility allows you to hear My words as truth and accept your holiness and righteousness found in Me independent of your actions.

Fruit is not the avoidance of a behavior. Fruit is intentionally grown and given away for others to enjoy and gain strength and nourishment. Fruitfulness is not the absence of sin. To bear fruit is to abide in Me morning, noon, and night; to allow My words and perspectives, love, and power to flow through the vessel that is you.

Stop viewing yourself or others as good or bad, right or wrong! Do not focus on or try to be good. Focus on Me and Me alone. That is where goodness flows from. I am the Way, the Truth, and the Life! Apart from Me, you can do nothing.

Whatever you do in your life apart from Me will not be eternal. You must seek to follow and abide in Me in everything you say and do so that it has eternal consequences. Being eternally minded means putting every view, every perspective, every thought, every word, and every action through the Father, Son, and Holy Spirit. It starts slow, but as you grow in your love and knowledge of the Lord then it becomes second nature because We have made our home inside of you. You are a temple of God, hosting the presence of the Lord. That is who you are.

1 Corinthians 6:19-20 "Or do you not know that your body is a temple of the Holy Spirit within you, whom you have from God? You are not your own."

61

WORSHIP INTO VICTORY

P salm 62:5 "For God alone, O my Soul, waits in silence, for my hope is from Him."

Before a battle, the Israelites would raise their banners and worship in preparation for the fight before them, reigning their focus in on the Lord Almighty, not the enemy or the task at hand. "The Lord will fight for you, you have only to be still" (Exodus 14:14). I will wait for you, Lord. My victory is in you, the King of Kings. "But thanks be to God, who gives us the victory through our Lord Jesus Christ" (1 Corinthians 15:57).

"But thanks be to God, who in Christ always leads us in triumphal procession, and through us spreads the fragrance of the knowledge of Him everywhere. For we are the aroma of Christ to God among those who are being saved and among those who are perishing, to one a fragrance from death to death, to the other a fragrance from life to life" (2 Corinthians 2:14-16).

Victory comes through worship. Worship shifts our focus from the problem, the enemy, and from our flesh, onto God. Whatever we focus on we empower. The thoughts and images that come to mind when we think about God may very well be the most important thing in our lives. Worship opens our hearts and minds, and increases faith, to see God as he is: the all-powerful, all-knowing Creator of the universe.

All things are held together through Him (Colossians 1:17). Worship opens our hearts to see the victory God has already set before us and the provision he has attached to the problem to carry us into the appropriation of that victory. In other words, he has already seen and provided for the victory, our job is to align with him and step into it. We worship into victory.

62

WHAT A GLORIOUS NIGHT

Luke 2:13-14 "And suddenly there was with the angel a multitude of the heavenly hosts praising God and saying, 'Glory to God in the highest, and on earth peace among those with whom he is pleased."

A spirit of revelation came upon Michelle and me listening to this song. That means something "clicked" and all of a sudden what we had known to be a great time of the year, Jesus's birth, became real in a new fresh way in our lives. That is, a true joy and excitement birthed within us as we thought about all of heaven rejoicing at Jesus' birth because they knew the season that was starting.

They knew that love had come, the Way, the Truth, and the Life. They knew that God had come down to earth in human form and the earth and everyone in it was going to be changed forever. The shepherds got this same revelation through the worship of the heavenly hosts because they couldn't help but go tell everyone what they had seen and heard.

This is a change in our spiritual lens, our perspective of how we view the coming and birth of Jesus. Taking an eternal perspective and seeing and experiencing as all of heaven sees and experiences. The Holy Spirit gives us revelation to see as He sees. It's to know Him more. To share in what He sees. It's to share in the joy and excited anticipation of His plans and purposes that are always good!

What a Glorious Night (a song by The Sidewalk Prophets)

63

TIME

God redeems our time. He makes a way when there is no way. He provides where the numbers don't add up. He redeems the lives of his servants (Psalm 34:22). He makes time when there are not enough hours in the day. He facilitates the completion of tasks in his timing, which is not bound to our logic.

God is not bound by time. He is simultaneously present in the past, present, and future. He concurrently lives in all situations. He does not dwell or operate under time constraints. But the enemy does. Lucifer is a finite created being, restricted to time just as we are.

Some of his tactics are to deceive us into wasting time, for he knows that his time is short (Revelation 12:12). He feeds us lies about God's authority and completeness over time, and he presents time as an obstacle to overcome, rather than a gift.

Our time on this earth is but a vapor, a mist (James 4:14) with a specific purpose. See, we are his workmanship, created in Christ Jesus for good works which he prepared beforehand that we should walk in them (Ephesians 2:10). God has a plan and purpose, a destiny for each of us.

Satan, the world, and our flesh like to persuade us we must do it all perfectly, and then do more. They love to put pressure, in both time and performance, on our shoulders. False expectations that detract from God's complete and beautiful intentions for you and me.

John says in John 3:27, "a person cannot receive even one thing unless it is given him from heaven." By his divine power, God has given us everything we need for living a godly life. We have received all of this by coming to know Him, the One who called us to himself by means of his marvelous glory and excellence (2 Peter 1:3, NLT).

Father already knows the beginning from the end. He has a solution in mind for every problem, and the provision to accompany it. Perceived problems steal time from us, causing stress and frustration, worry, and anxiety.

Recognition of process trusts God's goodness in every situation, believing He works all things for good, wastes no opportunity, and always speaks and moves at just the right time. We shift our perspective in time from problems to process.

Bill Johnson says it this way, "your faith can only function where you know Him to be good. Your faith will only explore where you have an essence of his goodness." We have choices and options in our time because we serve a God who is extremely good all the time, in all times, every time, and is completely unbound by time.

64

EMBRACING LIMITATIONS

Open your heart and mind to see and hear and think and speak with the mind of Christ (1 Corinthians 2:16), in the way of the Lord.

You are the branches (John 15:5), living under the limitations and growth of the Vine and Vinedresser. The branch has no awareness of the reason, direction, speed, or even the purpose of its growth until it happens and fruit is grown.

The branch can produce nothing of itself, nor can it determine what fruit it will bear or when it will bear fruit. The branch is at the whim of the Vine and the Vinedresser. The branch's purpose, growth, and development are determined by the Vine and the Vinedresser.

Jesus is the Vine and the Father is the Vinedresser. Whoever abides in Him, Jesus will bear much fruit, but apart from Him, one can do nothing.

A man can receive only what is given him from heaven (John 3:27). When what heaven gives us does not meet our personal desires, sometimes selfish and prideful, then we are frustrated, or discontent, jealous, or sometimes seek our own gain outside of Christ.

When we fail to embrace our limitations and rather live in entitlement that we should have more or a higher status, or have a certain position, we have become our own god, seeking what heaven has not given. As a branch, we are attempting to bear fruit and grow independently of the Vine. We fail to abide in Jesus and instead are abiding in selfish and prideful desires.

We must decrease, He must increase (John 3:30). Not our will but His will be done. We must embrace our limitations, allowing the sting of the Father's gentle humility to saturate our hearts, our minds, and the way we think and act. We must decrease, He must increase.

Our contentment comes in abiding in Jesus, through the love and power and fruit of the Holy Spirit, independent of our position or status before men. Limitations remind us of our humanity, that we are creatures created from dust by the Great and Mighty Eternal God of the universe.

We are not in control, God is. Limits help us to abide in Jesus, depend on the Holy Spirit, and kneel in surrendered submission before the Father. He must increase, we must decrease. A man can receive only what is given Him from heaven.

AUTHOR'S NOTE

These devotionals originated in the heart of the Father in 2012. Since that time, He and I have been crafting these during our morning times together. Sometimes a title would come to mind and as I wrote, the words flowed. Other times a topic would arise, usually one the Holy Spirit was walking me through during a season, and again, the words flowed.

These have come from my journal entries over the past 10 years. I would share them with other men, friends, small groups, from time to time. It was not until about eighteen months ago that I knew their primary purpose. The Holy Spirit began to convict me about stewarding what he had given me through these devotionals.

My first act of obedience was to call my pastor and offer them as a free resource for the church. As I began to consolidate them, I believed God wanted more. I initiated the journey of self-publishing as an act of obedience. My prayer is that God places this book in the right hands of the right people at the right time so that it will bless and transform the hearts of millions.

I believe God has breathed on these words, manifesting the truth of Jesus's statement in John 6:63; His words are spirit and life. Let me be clear, this does not mean everything is correct. I am not attempting to teach or create theology, and God has brought me into new experiences with Him since this project began. But I have left entries that I might look at differently today as we continually grow and mature in our perspective of ourselves and the Lord. I hope that each of us as lifelong disciples have the freedom to learn new truths about the Lord, His ways, and ourselves. It doesn't always mean the former ways of thinking were wrong, it confirms his promise to continually reveal new mysteries and upgrade our minds. I pray that you will open your heart to what the Holy Spirit wants to speak to and transform in your life. Enjoy being with the Father. Find and enjoy him, for that is what I did writing these. I enjoyed listening to and being with our beautiful Savior, Master, King and Friend.

Thank you … grace and peace.

Printed in the United States
by Baker & Taylor Publisher Services